War Stories

War Stories

Compiled
by

Art Giberson

FOREWORD

Despite all the great accomplishments mankind made during the 20th century—invention of the automobile, the airplane, nuclear-power, space flight, putting a man on the moon and numerous advancements in medicine and science—the 20th century, in all likelihood, will be recalled by future historians as a century of war.

From the American Revolutionary War to the present American military personnel, conscripts and volunteers, have placed their lives on the line in the name of freedom. The personal story of each of those warriors is different—yet they are the same. These are the stories of the heroes who fought America's battles— personal stories that need to be preserved for future generations.

The material for *War Stories* was conceived as a series of personal World War II accounts, told by wartime veterans, for publication in a small weekly newspaper. A brief announcement for veterans who would like to participate in the series was published in the newspaper a couple of weeks before the planned commencement date. The response from World War II veterans wanting to tell their story was such a huge success that each of the paper's four staff members were assigned a list of veterans to interview. The list included officers and enlisted men and women from all branches of the armed forces. They had served as infantrymen, aviators, submariners, combat photographers, cooks, supply technicians, gunners and engineers.

Included in the group were several former prisoners of war— one of which spent the entire war as a POW in Japan. Another participant was a member of the Women's Royal Australian Air Force who later migrated to the United States as a war bride. A World War II widow tells of the cruel circumstances of her husband's death at the hands of the enemy while being held as a prisoner of war.

The 18-part World War II series was so well received by the newspaper's readers that it was decided to extend the series to include Korea, the Cuban Missile Crises, Vietnam and the Gulf War. They too proved to be an equally big hit with readers—particularly military history buffs. Each of the separate war story sequences received praise from numerous veterans groups and received several journalistic citations; including top journalism awards from the Navy and Department of Defense.

The men and women interviewed for the Korea, Vietnam and Desert Storm sequences, like their War World II counterparts, served in every field. They ranged in rank from private to generals and admirals — regular military, Reservists and National Guardsmen. These were and are America's finest — the sons, daughters, brothers, sisters, mothers and fathers, who gladly went in harm's way to ensure that freedom prevails.

Sadly, several of the veterans who shared their stories for this narrative have fought their last skirmish and now rest in peace.

ACKNOWLEDGEMENTS

Heartfelt appreciation is extended to the many warriors featured in this book. The stories of their wartime experiences are a true legacy that deserves to be preserved for future generations. They came from throughout the United States in response to their country's call to arms. They are true American heroes willing to go in harm's way for the benefit of all mankind.

Grateful appreciation is also extended to the reporters of a small weekly newspaper—Scott D. Hallford, Mike Antoine, Sheila K. Vemmer, Stacee James, Larry W. Kachelhofer—for their support and cooperation in compiling and preserving a slice of American history.

**This book is dedicated to the man and women of
America's Armed Forces...
Past, Present and Future**

WORLD WAR II

1941-1945

Roy S. Whitcomb:

Encounter with a Wolf

Retired Navy Commander Roy S. Whitcomb came a long way from poverty to a distinguished naval career. Mired in the lingering effects of the Great Depression, Whitcomb worked while in high school as a paper delivery boy for the *Jacksonville* (Florida) *Journal* before school making $3.50 a week. He supplemented that income by working on weekends from 7 a.m. to midnight at an A&P for $1.50 a day and all the over-ripe bananas he could eat.

Despite the economic hardships and arduous schedule Whitcomb still managed to play high school football and graduated in June 1935. That same year, he applied for enlistment in the Navy and was accepted in June 1936.

After completing boot camp at Norfolk, Virginia, he was assigned to the USS Nitro, an ammunition supply ship, then in dry dock for overhaul. "The most memorable events I have of the time were good chow and reasonable living quarters," Whitcomb said. "The most unpleasant memory was that it was a very harsh winter that year and I once had wool gloves on that froze while scraping barnacles from the ship."

After overhaul of the Nitro, he was assigned to the USS Chaumont, a transport ship, which had orders to the Pacific Fleet.

After a near unbearable winter in Norfolk, Whitcomb said he really enjoyed the trip to San Diego via the Panama Canal and the warm temperatures.

"Although warm, the ship was loaded with a couple thousand Navy and Marine recruits. En route, we experienced some pretty rough weather. And I can distinctly recall that the forecastle deck was covered with retching, seasick personnel who had not yet established their 'sea legs.' Fortunately, I didn't have that trouble."

Having taken typing in high school, Whitcomb was temporarily assigned to the ship's personnel office. This put him in position to get first shot at some of the best orders. All the recruits on board were to be dispersed to various assignments within the fleet. Whitcomb said the personnel officer advised him that the best assignment would be to one of the bigger ships in the fleet—a battleship or a carrier. "I chose the USS Lexington (CV-2) home ported at Long Beach, California."

He spent two years on the Lexington, the first as a member of the deck force. He later became a radioman and was assigned to the Carrier Division Two staff at North Island.

Then he was assigned to VS-2, one of the Lexington's air group squadrons as a radioman/gunner. After about 200 hours in the back seat of dive-bombers, he got a chance to take some leave and visit his family back in Florida. "I met a charming, delightful young lady who was a family acquaintance," he said. He and Ruby were married a year later, December 29, 1939, as war clouds grew stormy over Europe.

"I was debating ending my Navy career to spend more time with my bride, but things in Europe were heating up and I knew we would be getting involved. So I decided I would stay in under the condition that I could go through flight training."

Whitcomb reported to Pensacola, Florida (the Cradle of Naval Aviation) and completed flight training as a Naval Aviation Pilot (NAP) in May 1942. Now a chief petty officer, he was assigned to multi-engine aircraft, which he initially didn't like. "I was very disappointed because my beloved Lady Lex had been sunk in the Coral Sea," he said. "I wanted to fly fighter aircraft so I could get out there and chew them up."

He was ordered to VP-74 where he flew the Martin PBM-3 Mariner, a patrol bomber seaplane primarily responsible for anti-submarine warfare. "The Mariner was a radically different plane that had a large number of NAPs assigned to them." NAPs were assigned to the Mariners because they were new, complicated weapons systems, and the enlisted aviators had backgrounds in structural mechanics, electronics and a great deal of naval experience.

VP-74 was operating off the coast of South America in 1943 and Whitcomb had been promoted to lieutenant junior grade. German U- boats were taking their toll on Allied shipping concerns all through the Atlantic and South America was no different. One boat in particular, U-513, was having a very good summer.

On June 21, the U-513 sank the Swedish vessel SS Venezia. Later that month, a Brazilian freighter was sunk.

On July 3, the liberty ship Elihu B. Washburne went down. U-513 continued its terror with torpedoes July 16 when it sank a U.S. freighter. The captain told the survivors from the freighter he'd spent seven years in Brooklyn and asked how the Dodgers were doing.

Earlier, on July 7, Whitcomb had seen a U-boat but it crash-dived before he had a chance to attack it.

On July 19, U-513 surfaced to radio Berlin. The captain said in the message that he thought Allied air patrols against the U-boats were ineffective and more subs should be sent. For the skipper of U-513, that proved to be an ill-fated call. Whitcomb, piloting a Mariner, and his crew were homing in on the U-513.

"After we got close and spotted them, I kept flying straight in some low clouds so they would think that we hadn't seen them," he said. "But then a hail of gunfire rose from the deck of the sub.

"I came in out of the sun to have an advantage. I was trying to avoid the fire but went on and dropped Mark 44 depth charge bombs. Two landed on either side of the sub and two ran up to the bow."

Whitcomb had dropped his bombs from an altitude of 50 feet and only a few seconds after the explosions he looked back at the sub and it was gone. Only a few survivors were seen in the water.

"Most of the people who survived were the ones who had been on deck operating the guns," he said. "When we came back around I ordered a 10-man life raft to be dropped. We made a second pass and estimated there were 15-20 survivors and made another pass to drop life jackets."

Whitcomb stayed on station circling the survivors for two hours until relieved by another Mariner. Several hours later, the USS Barnegat picked up the German U-boat survivors.

U-513 was kaput, but the captain, Kapitanleutenant Frederich Guggenberger, who had inquired about the Dodgers and called allied anti-sub patrols a joke was rescued.

Whitcomb was responsible for the capture of Germany's most famous U-boat commander. Guggenberger was renowned in Hitler's dreaded U-boat "wolf packs." In 1941 he was decorated by Hitler with the Iron Cross for sinking the British aircraft carrier HMS Ark Royal.

While Guggenberger was recovering in sick bay, he asked if he could meet his foe who bettered him. Whitcomb accepted and went to see his enemy. "He spoke excellent English and said if his U-boat had surfaced five minutes earlier, his crew would have shot us down," said Whitcomb. "But he also said I made a very good attack on him."

Whitcomb said he met then-Admiral Guggenberger 15 years later in Germany, by then an ally of the United States. Guggenberger had also by that time attended the U.S. Naval War College in Rhode Island.

Whitcomb and his crew became celebrities of sorts for a while, but the war dragged on and Whitcomb was back in the cockpit. At the end of the war in Europe, VP-74 was sent to the Galapagos Islands to protect the Panama Canal from the Pacific side. VP-74 had been responsible for six German sub kills in the Atlantic and a NAP was at the controls in each victory.

Whitcomb's career took him too many different places and into various jobs/projects. But the two he is most proud of was a program to educate enlisted members of the advantages of making the Navy a career and the establishment of the Naval Flight Officer program. Whitcomb retired from the Navy in 1971.

###

Robert C. Wagner:

One of the Crazy Ones

Their images have appeared in films, books and magazines. Much of what the world knows about World War II (and most other 20th century wars and conflicts) is the product of a unique group of warriors responsible for documenting American battlefield activities in Europe and the Pacific during World War II—combat photographers.

Without the heroism and courage of the men and women who choose to go to war armed only with cameras, the sacrifices made by American servicemen and women would largely go undocumented. One of the men responsible for the world's huge reservoir of World War II images is Robert C. Wagner—the Navy's most decorated World War II photographer.

Wagner, a Cumberland, Maryland, native, joined the Navy shortly after graduating from high school in 1937.

"I had gotten a job with a photo studio but I didn't know a whole lot about photography when I answered an ad in a newspaper. But I figured my enthusiasm and desire to learn would make up for my lack of knowledge...It almost worked," Wagner laughed, recalling how he talked his way into a job as a photographer's assistant.

"I had only worked at the studio for a short while when the boss called me into his office and said, 'Kid you have more enthusiasm than anyone I've ever seen. When you learn a little more about photography come back and see me. I'll have a job for you.'"

I had heard that the Navy trained men to be photographers so off I went to the Navy recruiting office and enlisted. Much to my surprise, however, it was nearly two years before I finally reported to photo school. After recruit training I reported first to a fighter squadron at San Diego then transferred to a utility squadron. Finally, in June 1939, my desire to be a Navy photographer came true when I finally received my orders to report to Pensacola, Florida, for training as a Navy photographer.

During the next several years Wagner attended several specialized photographic courses and schools, including one conducted by *National Geographic* magazine, which helped prepare him for what was to come.

Shortly after the attack on Pearl Harbor on December 7, 1941, the Navy created a combat photographic section within the Office of Public Relations headed up by Lieutenant Commander Carlton Mitchell. Mitchell decided the best way to provide photographic coverage of the war, which would satisfy the needs of civilian and government sources, would be the creation of small, elite combat photographic units (CPU) capable of going anywhere on a moments' notice. Each unit consisted of four men; an officer and three enlisted photographers — one of which had to be a motion picture cameraman. Wagner was assigned to CPU-4.

"Our first action was the invasion of Attu, (at the end of the Aleutian chain), Wagner recalls. "We left Washington D.C. with our gear rather loose and unorganized. We went to Seattle by train and then rode a tanker to Dutch Harbor where we stayed for two weeks. We took advantage of the stay to build strong watertight wooden boxes for our equipment and supplies.

"Because we were a small mobile unit, we anticipated many fast transfers at sea, even in rough weather, so we made sure the boxes would float when fully loaded. Each box was identified, according to its contents and numbered so they could be left onboard a landing ship, with instructions that certain ones — those containing another supply of film for example — should be sent in to the beach master on the third day of the landing. We had everything under control and were ready for action...or so we thought," the silver-haired combat cameraman said with a far-away look as though in deep thought.

"I still have this vivid impression of our transfer to the USS Haywood, a troop carrier," Wagner said. "We were riding a tug, with our gear piled six-feet high, on the foredeck, waving our arms to attract attention because the ladders were being raised, and the anchor was grinding up.

"As we approached the ship we could hear the commanding officer a white-haired veteran of Pearl Harbor and the early Pacific action, bellowing from the bridge to the officer of the deck. 'Here come those damn photographers, they are going to want me to turn the ship around while we are trying to fight a war!' He mumbled a few unquotable facts about photographers in general, and then directed the duty officer to lower a ladder and take us aboard.

"The next day our officer-in-charge, Lieutenant Harold Tacker, called on the CO (commanding officer) and pointed out that we were there under his command, and that we did not expect him to turn the ship around or do any other special favors for us. Lieutenant Tacker told the captain that we also had a job to do. The pending invasion, Tacker told the captain, would be the first retaking of American soil and because the American people badly needed a victory it was going to be a very newsworthy event.

"Later that evening I gave the same pitch to several of the junior officers and chief petty officers. 'This ship,' I told them, 'has an outstanding war record. You have been in every major Pacific action; the crew hasn't had any leave or replacements for 18 months; the ship badly needs an overhaul; and your small boats need radar and other equipment.'"

"Tacker then proceeded to educate the CO about the value of publicity and ended up assuring him that with a minimum of cooperation we would be able to feature the Haywood and its activities, looming out of the fog, in news reels and feature pictures throughout the United States.

"His ship, the lieutenant told the Haywood's captain, would get overhauled and the crew would get leave. That may have been a bit of a snow job, but it turned out to be pretty factual. We met some of the Haywood's crew later in the South Pacific and they had glowing stories about their 45 days of leave in the states.

"The Haywood's skipper, a commander when we went aboard, made captain and the ship was featured in a one hour film called 'The Yanks at Attu,' in nearly every theater in the United States.

During the two-week voyage to Attu, the Army held daily briefings. Two main landings were planned for the first day: one at the main Japanese camp at Holtz Bay and the other at Massacre Bay, a smaller installation with steep sloops on which the Japanese were well entrenched.

The photographers decided to go ashore just before daylight with the first wave at Holtz Bay. This would give the unit time to get in and set up before the heavy resistance began.

The Army wasn't exactly thrilled about having Navy photographers in the lead boats however. Lieutenant Tacker worked his way up the Army chain of command until he met the Army general in charge of the entire Attu operation. It turned out that the general was an enthusiastic amateur photographer, and after a discussion about "cold weather" photography, directed his chief-of-staff to see that his new Navy friends were well taken care of.

Wagner recalls that it was a 14-mile run into the beach. By 2 a.m. the weather had turned so bad that the small landing craft circling to load the troops got lost when they were only 30 yards from the ship. About 3 a.m., a destroyer was dispatched to lead the way to the beach.

The photographers didn't shoot much film on that wave, but by noon the weather had cleared somewhat and they returned to the Haywood to photograph the unloading operations and then went back ashore with the next wave of troops.

Following the Aleutians campaign, Wagner, a chief photographer's mate at the time, was reassigned and spent the reminder of the war flying combat photo missions. He covered nearly every major campaign in the Pacific and for his heroism was awarded the Air Medal, Legion of Merit and a chest full of lesser awards. By war's end Chief Wagner had the distinction of being the most decorated Navy photographer of World War II.

But of all the medals, ribbons and citations Wagner received he says his most cherished award was winning his combat air crew wings.

"Those wings mean more to me than all the other awards combined," he said.

The International Combat Camera Association has a motto which proclaims: "The Brave Ones Were Shooting Bullets. The Crazy Ones Were Shooting Film." Wagner, who retired from the Navy as a lieutenant commander qualifies as being both brave and yes, perhaps a little crazy.

###

Russell Sullivan

Coast Guardsman at War

New Haven, Connecticut, native son Russell Sullivan was making 65 cents an hour working for the post office. The year was 1934. Five years later Sullivan switched careers and went to work with the FBI. That was, followed by the first of two stints with the Treasury Department (U.S. Customs).

In 1942, life began to change for Sullivan when he applied for a commission with the Navy, Coast Guard and Marine Corps. "The Coast Guard accepted me," he says. "I considered that a major victory. I was anti-backpack carrier," he laughs. "I didn't want to go for long walks with a pack on my back." Sullivan received a direct commission based on oil pollution cases he had brought to court in Connecticut.

"The Coast Guard was looking for people under 25 who had legal backgrounds. When I was in Washington, D.C. (with the FBI) I attended Columbus University Law School for two years." Sullivan began his active duty career with the Coast Guard in port security, before attending officer indoctrination school in 1943 in St. Augustine, Florida. Later, as a newly promoted lieutenant (junior grade) Sullivan was put in command of CG-83342, an 83-foot sonar-equipped patrol boat, many of which were later used in the Normandy invasion.

"I wrote a letter to Coast Guard Headquarters and told them I wanted to get on a bigger ship."

His wish came true. Four hours later he was aboard the USS Aquarius (AKA-16), an attack cargo vessel. "The brass at headquarters was looking for a live one," he laughs. "I guess they found him, because that had to be the fastest set of orders ever written. The transfer to a larger ship also brought him a promotion to full lieutenant.

"While serving aboard the Aquarius we went from a dry dock in Brooklyn to San Francisco, via the Panama Canal, to pick up our cargo—a shipload of canned turkey bound for Pearl

Harbor— Sullivan and his shipmates participated in several Pacific campaigns, including Guam, Iwo Jima and Leyte.

Sullivan says one of his most vivid experiences came not too long before the dropping of the atomic bomb over Hiroshima, while he was serving aboard the Coast Guard-manned USS General Robert L. Howze (AP-134) which was crossing the shark-infested waters of the Pacific between the Philippines and Guam.

"I was the officer of the day and had just relieved the watch about noon when we came upon these bodies—blackened from sea oil. There were hundreds of them," he recalls vividly. "We asked a destroyer already on the scene if they needed any assistance, and the reply came back negative."

The Howze, which was headed for Manila with 4,000 troops from a division being redeployed from Europe, sailed through the tragedy, assuming it was a Japanese ship which had been sunk.

It wasn't until after the ship had been in Manila a short time that the crew of the Howze learned the shocking truth.

"The Howze's captain returned from the port director's office all red in the face," recalls the retired Coast Guard captain, "and called for an immediate meeting with all ship's officers and chief petty officers in the wardroom."

'I was informed,' began the captain, 'that the bodies we sailed through were from the USS Indianapolis. It was sunk by a Japanese submarine and hadn't been missed for four days.'

Somberly, Sullivan speculates on what might have happened if the Howze, which had sailed along the same track as the doomed cruiser, had encountered the same enemy sub.

"If they had hit us, we would have lost thousands of men. They were crammed in the ship like sardines, with bunks 18 inches apart and five to six high."

A half century after the war Sullivan remained justifiably upset that his ship, as well as the Indianapolis, wasn't afforded an escort, in

11

view of the evidence that Navy intelligence was aware of submarine activity in the area.

Another episode in the Pacific, which Sullivan recalls with humor, involved a downed Marine Corps flyer. "We were underway during one of the campaigns, and a Marine pilot in a Corsair went down in the water near us. We put a boat over the side and the plane stayed afloat long enough for the pilot to get out of it. When we got him aboard, one of our officers jokingly told him that he would have to pay for the airplane. The amusing part was... the pilot actually believed him!"

Another incident that stands out in Sullivan's memory is of 13 U.S. Marines being buried at sea off the coast of Guam. "We just couldn't bury them on land because the fighting was so severe," he recalls.

Sullivan was far away from the relative safety of port security, for which he had initially joined the Coast Guard but even port security can have its anxious moments. Sullivan recalls a close encounter experienced by one pier guard, John Cullen. "He was patrolling the beach one night," Sullivan recalls, "when he came up on five Germans who had landed from a submarine."

"The saboteurs decided not to kill the guard since he'd be missed right away," Sullivan said, "so they bribed him with a hundred dollars—five $20 bills. You have to remember; most enlisted sailors back then were only earning $30 a month." Sullivan says,

"The guard took the money and continued his patrol back to the life boat station. Reaching the station he requested that the petty officer of the watch get the chief up. The chief listened intently as Cullen related what had happened... thinking all the while that Cullen was screwy until he showed him the money.

"They got in a jeep and went back to where Cullen said he had seen the saboteurs and found where they'd buried their rubber suits and gear.

"The saboteurs, who were planning to blow up factories in the United States, were caught. Three were executed. Two, who had surrendered voluntarily, were given prison sentences.

Sullivan spent 38 years in the Coast Guard Reserve before retiring as a captain in 1976.

###

Norman Stutzer:

A scene right out of Hollywood

While most people consider the number 13 to be unlucky, retired Air Force Lieutenant Colonel Norman Stutzer considers 13 to be his lucky number.

In 1943, Stutzer, then a second lieutenant in the Army Air Corps, was assigned to the 94th Bomb Group flying B-17s from a remote air base in England. On Friday, Feb. 4, 1944, Second Lieutenant Stutzer and the crew of aircraft 013 took off to bomb the marshalling yards at Frankfurt am Main, Germany. About 45 minutes from the target, 013 was proceeding over the Ruhr Valley which Allied flyers had dubbed "flak valley" when it was hit by anti-aircraft fire. It was Stutzer's 13th mission over Germany.

So why does the World War II Army Air Corps veteran consider 13 to be his lucky number?

"Because I survived," says the retired lieutenant colonel without hesitation. Stutzer says he can still recall the bitter cold striking his face as he exited the aircraft. "We were at 23,000 feet. It was clear as a bell above, but directly below was a cloudbank. Falling toward the cloud bank, which seemed like an eternity, I remember looking up and seeing the rest of the formation flying overhead and thinking, 'Hey fellows! Don't fly off and leave me here.'"

Plunging through the thick layer of clouds, the young lieutenant landed in an open field. Unable to bury the chute, as he had been taught, because the ground was frozen, he scanned the area and spotted a small clump of woods nearby.

"I had just made it into the woods and was sitting on a log when I heard a twig snap," Stutzer remembers. "I ducked behind the log and held my breath. Peeking through a crack in the log, I saw a civilian with a shotgun coming in my direction. He walked up and propped his foot upon the log—the end of the shotgun only inches from my face. Man, that thing looked as big as a howitzer," Stutzer, said laughing.

"The German looked down and saw me. He jumped back and started frantically yelling and gesturing for me to get up and raise my hands. Pushing me along in front of him, I heard the shotgun go off and thought for sure I was dead."

After a moment or so several other German civilians joined them and Stutzer knew that the shot had been merely a signal. He was taken to a waiting truck where another American, apparently from one of the other aircraft in the bomb group, was being held. After a four or five-mile ride, the truck stopped in front of a garage where they were joined by two other Americans.

"A short time later I was taken from the group and led to the backdoor of a tavern. The door was opened and I was shoved into the middle of the room," the colonel recalls. "For a moment, I thought I was dreaming. It was a scene right out of Hollywood!

"On the wall there was a huge Nazi flag and a portrait of Hitler. The guard opened the front door. Outside was an icy walkway, about 50 feet long, with people lined up on both sides. At the end of the walkway was a car.

"As I walked toward the car, I was struck from both sides with rocks and sticks. When I reached the car someone handed me my parachute. Suddenly the civilians, who moments before were hitting me, were now helping me gather up the chute. Slipping and sliding on the ice, I returned to the tavern, escorted out the back door, and taken back to the garage. Like I said, it was like a scene right out of Hollywood."

Stutzer and his fellow POWs were next marched around the Town Square while townspeople yelled and threw things at them. "I was so cold and tired by this time that I really couldn't feel anything," the Harlem, New York, native recalls. After an hour or so of parading around the square the POWs were taken to the town jail where they were given coffee and a blanket and allowed to sleep.

"When I woke up it was dark. A German soldier opened the cell and took me to another room for interrogation. After giving my name, rank and date of birth, I was returned to the cell."

The next morning the POWs were put on a train and taken to an interrogation center near Frankfurt. Their shoes and personal belongs were taken away. They were then placed in solitary and given some bread and soup. Several days later Stutzer was taken before another interrogator.

"This guy looked like he was a model for a German Army recruiting poster." Stutzer said, "He wore an immaculate uniform complete with swastika armband and black, knee-length boots shined to a mirror-like gloss.

'What is the number of your airplane?' he asked. "I told him I couldn't remember. And, although I was expecting further and harsher questioning, he simply said, 'Go back to your room (cell) and think about it.' This little game continued for several days," Stutzer remembers. "Then one night the cell door was suddenly flung open and the interrogator asked in a very agitated voice, 'Have you thought of the number of your airplane yet?'

"Again I said no. He slammed the door shut and I heard him talking to someone outside the cell. The door opened again and a guard threw me my shoes. I had no doubt that they were going to take me out and shoot me. I walked out into the hallway and there stood the other three officers from my crew. This was the first time I had seen them since we had been shot down."

Stutzer and his fellow airmen were then moved to a holding area, given access to showers and issued clean GI-issue clothing, courtesy of the International Red Cross, and asked if they wanted their families to be notified. They were then transferred to a POW camp on the outskirts of Frankfurt—the date was Feb. 13, 1944.

A few months later, several hundred Allied POWs were taken from the camp, loaded into boxcars and transferred to a permanent camp, at Barth, Germany, where they remained for the next 16 months.

In the meantime, back home, Stutzer's wife, Mae, was notified that her husband had been shot down and missing in action. It would be four months before she learned of her husband's fate.

Even then her first information about her husband came not from the War Department, but by post card from a woman in Philadelphia, Pennsylvania.

"I frequently listen to shortwave radio broadcasts from Germany," the woman wrote, *"and I recently heard that your husband, Norman, had been captured. Thought I would pass the information on to you, in case you haven't heard."*

Hopeful, but apprehensive, Mae told some friends about the strange post card the next day at work where she worked as a censor in the Censor Office of the U.S. Post Office.

"Later that morning I went to the ladies room and my supervisor came in behind me and stuffed an envelope into my blouse. 'Read this,' she instructed, 'and give it back to me. It will be officially delivered tomorrow.'"

Retrieving the envelope, Mae opened it with trembling hands and quickly scanned the two-paragraph letter.

"Dear Mrs. Stutzer:
This office has received information that your husband, Second Lieutenant Norman Stutzer is being held as a prisoner of war.
The Provost Marshal General has directed me to inform you that Information we have been received indicates that his prisoner of war number is 2328. It is suggested that you use this number when addressing future correspondence to him."

Use the number she did. The first time Stutzer received mail from home, he got 58 letters from Mae. Most POWs received only two or three. Mae said, "I figured I worked for the Post Office, so I may as well take advantage of it."

During the 16 months he spent as a prisoner of war, Stutzer said the prisoners were mustered three times a day, allowed to receive Red Cross packages and given one lump of coal, per man, to burn for heat.

To help beat the boredom and pass time—in addition to looking for ways to escape—they devised numerous ways to keep busy, including printing a POW newspaper, copies of which the Stutzer family still has. But one of the keepsakes that Stutzer is proudest of is a plaque bearing the likeness of wings worn by the Allied airmen that were in his POW camp.

"Our Red Cross packages generally had canned meat or something of that nature in them," Colonel Stutzer recalls. "Now that was back in the days when most canned goods were sealed with a bead of solder around the edge of the can. What we would do is save that band and melt the solder off and use it to make different things. "I borrowed the wings worn by the other flyers, used them as a mold, and duplicated their wings. They made a real nice, one-of-a-kind plaque," Stutzer says gingerly presenting the plaque for inspection.

As time went by Stutzer said that bombing in the vicinity of the POW camp increased. "Everyone, including the POWs, knew the Allies were coming," said Stutzer. "So one night the guards just up and walked away. Not knowing what to expect, the senior POW decided we should just stay in the camp and wait for the Allies."

Finally on May 1, 1945, the camp was liberated by the Soviets. "Actually," Stutzer recalls, "the Soviets just walked into the camp. There was no one to stop them. A few days later we were sent to a RAMP (Repatriated Allied Military Personnel) camp in France for further processing."

With a German-sounding name, one of Stutzer's major concerns while in the RAMP was convincing the authorities that he really was an American. He and Mae were finally reunited in June 1945 when he arrived home for 60 days of leave.

Lieutenant Colonel Stutzer went on to serve in two other wars—Korea and Vietnam—before retiring from active military service in 1972.

#

Bill Shryock:

Close calls, Snipers and Miracle Soup

William "Bill" Shryock considers himself lucky. Heck, he considers the entire male population of his 1944 Wichita, Kansas, Augusta High School class very lucky.

"All of my classmates (76 in all) joined the military before we actually graduated high school. We graduated one day and left for service the next day. Amazingly, we all returned home intact after the war.

"We all went through boot camp together and nine of us stayed together until we got to the South Pacific."

After boot camp at the Naval Training Center, Great Lakes, Illinois, Shryock was assigned to the Naval Landing Force Equipment Depot at Guadalcanal as a third class storekeeper technician.

Recalling the voyage from New York City to the South Pacific, Shryock said "They were taking us to New York City across New Jersey and we saw the Queen Mary in the harbor. We thought 'Oh man, we're going to Europe aboard the Queen Mary!'

"What we didn't see from the bus, was a Kaiser Liberty ship, Empire Battle-Axe, right in front of the Queen Mary. We sailed on that thing for 45 days. From New York we sailed down the Atlantic Coast through the Panama Canal then on to the South Pacific."

"That thing was so filthy. But it was an experience—not a very good one, but one which I have never forgotten. There were so many men onboard that many of them had to sleep on the decks. And the food! I can't even start talking about that stuff," he laughs.

Shortly after Shryock and his colleagues debarked, the British-manned lend-lease ship was condemned, never to carry American troops again "And that was in the middle of the war," Shryock laughs. "The Empire Battle-Axe was sunk not long afterward by a Japanese sub."

On Guadalcanal, Shryock was part of the effort to outfit a planned invasion force of the Japanese mainland. Actually all of Shryock's experience on Guadalcanal weren't all bad. One experience he recalls fondly was Christmas 1944.

"My mom canned some chicken soup in a quart-sized glass jar and sent it to me on Guadalcanal. She packed it in popcorn, with probably 6 inches of padding all around it.

"We had an absolute feast." Shryock continues. "We also enjoyed some corn on the cob with the soup, courtesy of a nearby Army garden," he laughs. "Considering the way packages were handled during World War II, the safe arrival of the soup was a bit on the miraculous side."

There were also many close calls. One occurred while Shryock was on harbor patrol. "I had the 2200-0200 (10 p.m. - 2 a.m.) watch. There was this great, big full moon out—the Japanese weren't supposed to be around—and I was walking along a pile of skids. I sat down on 'em for just a second, then felt like I'd better get on with my patrol.

"It probably wasn't 10 minutes later and the whole heavens lit up and I got knocked down by the force of a tremendous blast. The Japanese had just sunk a docked ammo ship. The ship's entire complement— more than 200 men, were killed.

"When I went back to where I'd been sitting, the area was completely destroyed by the ship's anchor, which had been blown off the ship. Body parts washed ashore for weeks after that."

Shortly after that episode, Shryock's troop transport ship went island hopping, picking up personnel on the way for the push to Japan. During the voyage, the ship encountered the fury of Mother Nature. "Going from Guadalcanal to Okinawa we got caught in a typhoon. Our ship was like an ant in a bucket of water. The waves were 10 stories high and we all just knew the ship would never make it. Although every man aboard was aware of the danger, I guess we were just sorta immune to the idea of dying. You know that it happens in war, but it always happened to the other guy.

"Like the first night on Okinawa we were dug in and the Japanese were being chased right by us, and it was like 'why are you disturbing my sleep' type of thing."

Shryock's troop transport was en route to Japan when the 19-year-old and his shipmates learned about the utter destruction of two cities in Japan by atomic bombs. "We really cheered when we heard that, because then we knew the invasion of Japan would be called off and thousands of lives would be saved."

The ship was diverted to Okinawa, where he recalls movie-watching snipers. "We'd be watching movies in the camp and the Japanese soldiers who had not yet surrendered could hear the 'pow-pow-pow' from the screen.

"They'd sneak in and climb up in the trees, and instead of shooting they'd get absorbed in the movies. Our security guards would have to shoot 'em out of the trees."

Shryock stayed on Okinawa until his return home for Christmas 1945. Shryock's discharge from the Navy in June 1946 wasn't the end of his military service. Three years later he got a job with the U.S. Marine Corps as an inspector/instructor. In 1953 he received a commission as a second lieutenant in the United States Marine Corps. He later saw combat action in two other major armed conflicts—Korea and Vietnam.

Shryock retired from the Marine Corps in 1970 with the rank of major.

###

F. Worth Scanland II:

<u>Placing her in Harm's Way</u>

Some lives you can summarize in a few paragraphs. Some lives can fill a full newspaper page. And some lives fill volumes. The life of F. Worth Scanland II is one of the latter. The following is just a small portion of the extraordinary life led by one man.

F. Worth Scanland II was born to a Navy life. His father, Commodore Francis Worth Scanland, was skipper of the submarine O-11 when the young Scanland, age 10, stood on a banana crate and peered through the boat's periscope. From then on, Scanland's heart was set on becoming the skipper of his own submarine.

Following in the footsteps of his father, he attended the Naval Academy, served his two-year probationary period as an ensign and was immediately chosen to attend the Naval Submarine School in New London, Connecticut, in June of 1936.

After graduating from Submarine School, Scanland worked his way through several submarines, starting with the S-39, and then on to the Sea Dragon which had just returned from an overseas tour. Scanland's life changed once again.

Answering an early morning phone call during breakfast with his wife and two young sons at their home in Hawaii, Scanland learned of his next assignment. "Pack one suitcase and come down to headquarters. That's all I can tell you," said the voice on the other end of the line.

"They took me down to the dock at Pearl Harbor and there was the USS Tuna. They had lost their executive officer, and I was told to go—the engines were running. Sailors were standing by to pull up the gangway as soon as I crossed over. I didn't even have time to go to a phone and tell my wife 'Hey, I'm going. I don't know when I'll see you again.' You know, Navy wives really had it tough in those days."

After Scanland shook the skipper's hand, Tuna's gangway was pulled up and she shoved off. "We went to San Francisco, to Mare

Island, where they put the Tuna in dry dock. They had discovered that the torpedo tubes were misaligned," says Scanland.

"While in dry dock, the news of the Japanese attack on Pearl Harbor came in over the radio. My grandmother, mother, father, wife, sons— everyone in my family was there in Hawaii while I was sitting in dry dock, in the states—helpless."

Scanland soon received orders to the USS Peto as the prospective XO, and met up with the submarine in Manitowac, Wisconsin. Once commissioned, Peto made her long trip to sea, eventually arriving in Brisbane, Australia. Following her second war patrol, Scanland again received orders back to Manitowac, this time as the prospective commanding officer of the USS Hawkbill (SS-366).

The legacy of Scanland's command of Hawkbill is one filled with tradition, strength and valor, with a little bit of humor thrown in for good measure. From the moment the skipper watched his wife christen the ship with a champagne bottle, Scanland charged full speed ahead.

He was the only commanding officer Hawkbill ever had, and, according to a citation from the Task Force Board of Awards, "Few submarines have had a more auspicious record." He saw it through hull laying, war, and decommissioning.

Planning the commissioning party was part of Scanland's job as the new CO. "This was the last time most of us would see our wives, families and girlfriends until the end of the war. It was important to me that it be done first class—first class included a Navy band."

Unfortunately, Scanland ran into some problems with James C. Petrillo, president of the Chicago Musician's Union. Petrillo claimed that union musicians had to be used in place of the Navy band, a claim that was backed up by the Navy.

Petrillo and the union won the musical skirmish, but Scanland won the battle in the fight with the Chicago Musician's Union—a small insight into the success of his career to come. To appease the union he hired the civilian musicians and told them to set up in the basement of the facility where the party was being held. "I instructed my executive officer to lock the door and not allow any of them out until the party was over and to check to make sure they continued playing."

With the commissioning party now but a memory, Hawkbill began its war patrols. "During our third or fourth patrol, I've forgotten which; we learned of the loss of the Lagarto, a sister boat, as the result of her submerged attack upon a small enemy convoy in the Gulf of Siam. This convoy was under the escort of H.I.J.M.S. Hatsutaka, a large destroyer with mine laying capabilities.

"When I was given this terrible news, I composed a message back to headquarters at Pearl Harbor requesting permission for Hawkbill to divert from her patrol orders and seek revenge for Lagarto's loss," says Scanland. "To my amazement, ComSubPac approved our request."

"Being situated close to the equator, it was often quite warm aboard the boat. I was asleep in my cabin," said Scanland, "when the emergency buzzer from the bridge brought me to my feet in one jump. I was into the passageway and control room, and half-way up the ladder to the conning tower before I realized I was totally naked."

It was too late for Scanland to turn around and get dressed, so he made his way to the bridge. With the crew at battle stations and the target bearing dead ahead, Scanland ordered the firing of a three "fish" spread.

"At the calculated time we heard and saw that wonderful flash and roar of a hit, and a shout went through the boat. We knew we had badly wounded her, but she didn't appear to be mortally hurt."

Hatsutaka immediately returned gunfire, and the Hawkbill pulled clear. (A young Sailor discreetly mentioned his state of undress to the skipper, and Scanland eventually dressed.) Still dark, the submarine waited until dawn to submerge, then surveyed the situation via periscope.

"What we observed was clearly our destroyer, lying broadside to us, dead in the water but otherwise apparently fully afloat." Scanland then observed a small float plane and a small power vessel approaching the wounded ship. "The urgency of putting Hatsutaka on the bottom quickly became apparent lest we lose her to a tow line.

"By this time the target had drifted in such a way that between it and the submarine was a large allied mine field, preventing us from get any closer than 5,000 yards. The maximum range at slow speed setting for the torpedoes the sub was carrying was 5,000 yards.

"We had no choice but to try, so I ordered a bow tube made ready. Closing as near as we dared to a torpedo run of 4,930 yards, I took aim at the space between the Hatsutaka's two smokestacks and fired one fish.

"The run time was calculated to be just under five minutes, and I glued my eye to the periscope every seemingly eternal minute of that five minutes, the track of the fish was clearly visible as it skidded on its way. I watched with great delight as that beautiful torpedo smacked into the port side of our enemy. With a mighty roar and huge geyser of sea water, Hatsutaka broke in two and joined our lost friends aboard Lagarto on the bottom of the Gulf of Siam."

"For about 30 minutes we tried everything possible to capture (rescue) an officer or sailor, but not a single one would allow himself to be taken, choosing instead to drown himself."

The crew may not have captured a human, but they managed to snag a life-ring inscribed "H.I.J.M.S. Hatsutaka" in English letters. "That life- ring now hangs in the Submarine Museum located in Manitowac, Wisconsin, the birthplace of the USS Hawkbill."

Avenging the loss of Lagarto was possibly the only occasion in U.S. naval history wherein one of its men-of-war deliberately set out to avenge the loss of a sister ship to the enemy and succeeded in achieving that objective.

Scanland sees another significant historical event in his reign aboard Hawkbill. "It was and probably will forever be the first and last attack by one naval man-of-war upon another during which the skipper was "buck nekked!"

Hawkbill survived five war patrols, including one where the submarine was "thoroughly, thoroughly depth charged," according to Scanland.

"We were lucky to ever surface after that." But on she fought. "Every patrol had its exciting moments," states Scanland. "Nobody, not one person ever showed the slightest sign of cracking up," he says of his crew. "They were just superb."

Throughout his career, Scanland gained the respect and admiration of many people, including the famous animator Walt Disney, who designed the ship's logo for Hawkbill. Once retired from the Navy, he continued expanding his horizons while still holding naval traditions and values close to his heart. Beneath the exterior of the calm-natured, self-described Navy retiree continues to beat the heart of a true naval man-of-war.

At the end of the war, Scanland and his father were both awarded the Navy Cross for their efforts—possibly the only father/son duo to do so at the time. Fleet Admiral Chester Nimitz pinned the cross on Scanland's tunic for bringing Hawkbill and her stalwart crew back home to San Francisco in one piece after, in the words of John Paul Jones at the commissioning of the Bonhomme Richard, "placing her in harm's way."

An excerpt from Hawkbill's Navy Unit Commendation reads: "Throughout five consecutive, highly successful war patrols Hawkbill sought out the enemy and attacked at every opportunity. With grim determination and repeatedly in the face of severe enemy counter measures, her valiant officers and crew attacked... sinking and damaging 21 ships totaling 40,900 tons. The valiant fighting spirit of the officers and men of this ship is an inspiration to all submarine personnel and in keeping with the highest traditions of the Naval Service."

###

John Rutledge:

Musician, Photographer, Pilot

For many, World War II memories come from movies, music, books, television... pop culture. But for those who were in Europe and the Pacific during World War II, the memories are all too real.

"Well, it was not very nice. Sometimes it brings back a lot of memories that you'd like to forget," says retired Lieutenant Commander John Rutledge. "But I think people should know about it. But they should also understand that there's no romance to war. None whatsoever."

Rutledge, who began his Navy career as a musician, was at his first duty station when the United States entered the war. "I was aboard the battleship USS California, getting ready to play colors at 8 o'clock," he says. "At 7:55, we heard a bunch of airplanes—which wasn't unusual—we were right beside the Ford Island Airfield at Pearl Harbor.

"But the tone of the propellers changed, and we knew that something was happening. We turned and looked around, but didn't see anything because of the cloud cover. Suddenly, an airplane came down through the clouds, pulled up and we saw what we thought, was a bomb drop. The first bomb, if that's what it actually was, never exploded, and we were unprepared for what followed. A second airplane came down through the clouds and dropped a bomb which exploded on a hangar.

"At about that time, we noticed the red meatball symbol on the wing of the airplane. The Japanese were attacking Pearl Harbor.

"The ship immediately sounded general quarters (GQ). We were tied up at Fox Four-right next to the air station itself. As soon as GQ sounded, the ship came alive, but it was tied to the pier with the electrical connections. Moments later, the ship was hit by two torpedoes in rapid succession.

"The ship bounced upward as the torpedoes exploded. Most of the people in the band, including me, were thrown over the side from the sudden rise of the ship. The torpedoes apparently hit the oil bunkers, and the oil seeped out into the harbor and quickly caught fire. It was, to say the least, a rather hectic moment."

The musician didn't know it at the time, but both of his ankles were broken in the chaos.

"I had old clodhopper high top shoes on, laced all the way up, and tied tight. When I got over to Ford Island, they had thrown a rope down from the ferry slip, and I went up the rope and made my way to the photo lab. The photo lab people knew that I was a photographer (Rutledge had been an avid photographer before he enlisted), so as soon I got there I was handed a K-20 (aerial camera) and two 50-foot rolls of film, and told go!"

"When he arrived in Hawaii for duty aboard the California, his first duty station, one of his stops was the base photo lab. I told them that I had some photographic experience and if I was needed I could work with them. Anybody who had experience, they were happy to have," says Rutledge. "So photography became my secondary job."

Many of the pictures that Rutledge has in a scrapbook were taken that day. He's not quite sure which photos are his though; the tumultuous environment that they were taken in led to a great deal of confusion.

Finishing off the film he was given, Rutledge was assigned to yet another collateral duty. "I was very fortunate, I had a federal government driver's licenses that allowed me to drive any type of vehicle that the Navy had," says Rutledge. "So, they put me in a two-and-a-half-ton truck after I ran out of film."

Rutledge spent the next three days transporting the wounded to the hospital and delivering machine guns and ammunition. "I never got out of the truck for three days," says Rutledge. "...Slept in the truck when I had a chance, ate a sandwich now and then, and must have drink several gallons of coffee."

When Rutledge finally exited the truck, he was in for a nasty surprise. "I hadn't realized that I had broken my ankles until I got out of the truck... and fell down."

"Everything was all torn to pieces. The Arizona, the West Virginia, the California—all of them were sunk," says Rutledge.

When the fighting had calmed, our commanding officer decided that it was useless to have musicians," laughs Rutledge. "The entire band, which by sheer luck, had all survived, were taken to the intelligence center. They put us into what was called JICPOA (Joint Intelligence Center, Pacific Ocean/Air). These were the people who later broke the Japanese code which allowed us to win most of the battles in the Pacific."

All the band members, except for the leader, who was a chief, were seaman first class Rutledge explains. "When they transferred us over to JICPOA, they immediately advanced us in rank and assigned us a different specialty. All 26 members of the band, except for me, were made first class yeomen."

"This is where I got myself into trouble," says Rutledge somewhat sarcastically. "Knowing that I was a photographer, they made me an intelligence photographer, and sent to places that I had no idea even existed."

"I spent the next 18 months in China taking pictures of unbelievable atrocities that the Japanese were performing on the Chinese." Rutledge is not at ease speaking of this assignment. He casts his eyes downward for a moment, and then looks up into the distance. Somberly, he continues. "Those were the most horrible things in the world—the Japanese had performed just absolutely the cruelest things that I ever saw in my life." Rutledge speaks quietly, haltingly. He doesn't finish his thoughts—it's as if he doesn't want the words to be spoken aloud. "I got so sick time, after time, after time, that I just had to turn around and walk off."

"I don't know what happened to most of the pictures I took during the war, but I hope none of them were ever displayed or published. The atrocities that the Chinese endured from the Japanese were just absolutely atrocious. Some people knew what was going on, but I don't think it ever became public knowledge. Anyway, all of the film shot during that period was sent to Washington D.C., so I never got to see it at all."

He didn't have to. Each and every photograph is placed indelibly in his mind, enhanced by the sounds, smells, and senses.

From musician to photographer, Rutledge took his next step toward yet another change in direction. "I had heard, while I was going back and forth from China to Pearl Harbor, that there was a program that allowed enlisted men to apply for flight training. So, during one my trips back to Pearl Harbor I put in for flight training."

In December 1943, the musician/photographer received the news—he had been accepted for flight training.

It was during flight training in Louisiana that Rutledge met his future wife, Juanita. "She was a student there also. I met her in January of 1944, and married her in July," Rutledge says with an easy grin.

After receiving his wings as a naval aviator, Rutledge was ordered to Kaneohe Bay, Hawaii. That's where he was when the war ended. "I was elated, naturally, just one of those things that—well, how do you explain it? You go out and expect to get yourself shot, or never come back, and then suddenly it's all over."

After flying for about a year as an enlisted pilot, Rutledge received a commission.

Rutledge doesn't dwell on his experiences during World War II. But ask him about the music of that era, and his eyes light up. He brings out an album packed with photos. Young sailors with painted upright basses, saxophones and trumpets posture for the cameras; their white "Dixie cups" perched jauntily on the backs of their heads.

"To me, that's the only kind of music. Artie Shaw brought his band to Hawaii and his piano player, Claude Thornhill was my idol. I happened to be back in Pearl when they were playing." Rutledge leans back and smiles, a fiery sparkle in his eyes.

There are two almost identical, 8x10 photos slipped between the pages of the worn album. They are portraits of bands representing two of the ships that were docked at Pearl Harbor on December 7, 1941. Rutledge recalls a battle of the bands competition held the night before the attack. "The winner hadn't been decided yet, but after the Japanese bombed us, we decided on them." Rutledge, says, pointing to the photo of the Sailors with a large A on their bandstand—the Sailors of the USS Arizona.

###

Alfred P. McCracken:

A Tiger by the Tail

Waves from the English Channel lapped the shore. The explosions and gunfire had subsided. Hundreds of bodies were strewn on the beach the morning after the attack.

The survivors have always been relatively reluctant to talk about the experience. Alfred P. McCracken, a motor mechanic on board the landing ship LST-511, is one of those survivors.

"I enlisted in 1943 when I was 17 and went to diesel school. I was in the Navy about six months and I was a second class petty officer."

McCracken was assigned to LST-511, which left Boston in March 1944 for England, one of thousands of ships that would be needed for the invasion of France. LST-511 and McCracken were part of Convoy T-4.

T-4, in addition to LST-511, was comprised of LSTs 58, 289, 496, 499, 507, 515 and 531. There were a total of about 5,000 soldiers and sailors in T-4. The LSTs were also packed with ammunition, fuel, vehicles and other equipment.

Of the 5,000 troops, nearly 800 died when the convoy was attacked by German E-boats, similar to U.S. Navy PT boats, during Exercise Tiger, a rehearsal for the June 6, 1944 invasion of Normandy.

"The convoy had departed from Plymouth and Brixham harbors. We were to sail into the English Channel then loop back for a mock landing on the beaches of southern England.

At about 2 a.m. April 28, 1944, the convoy was attacked. I don't remember hearing the explosions down in the engine room, but we were getting word from the bridge as to what was going on," McCracken recalled.

At about 2:30 a.m., the men of LST-511 heard a sickening metal- against- metal scraping under the ship. A torpedo that didn't detonate had hit them. However, within an hour, the German torpedoes sank two of the LSTs in the convoy and a third was badly damaged. Additionally, in the confusion, McCracken's LST was fired on by its sister LSTs, wounding 15 sailors and soldiers.

"We didn't give a whole lot of thought to the other ships being hit," he said. "When you're young like that you don't have the kind of fear you do later in life and realize what could have happened. We just figured we wouldn't be one of the ships torpedoed."

But the injuries incurred from friendly fire were severe enough for the ship to make for land to remove the wounded.

"One of the most seriously wounded was our executive officer who lost an eye," McCracken explained. "The skipper was hit in the leg with shrapnel and the communications officer was injured. And we had a coxswain on the bow that was wounded really bad."

Many of those who died from the other LSTs drowned or were burned to death from explosions onboard the ammunition and fuel-laden ships.

The E-boats made their way back to bases in France, leaving hundreds of dead that would wash up on the shores of England later in the morning.

Because security was so tight prior to D-Day, McCracken and all the others involved in Exercise Tiger were admonished from talking of the disaster. And he like many of the other survivors went on to participate in D-Day.

Those who were able returned to LSTs for the invasion. LST-511 got orders for landings on Omaha Beach.

"We loaded our troops in England on June 2. We had a captain onboard in charge of the task force," he said. "As we were heading toward France we got a coded message, 'post mike one,' which meant a one-day delay. The captain said, 'I've read all about this stuff and I thought I had everything planned, but I'll be damned if I know how to turn around and go back.'"

That was June 5. On June 6, McCracken's task force, part of the largest amphibious operation in history with a 6,000-ship armada, delivered troops to invade the continent of Europe.

"When we arrived at Omaha (Beach) on D-Day there was confusion," he said. "Because of that, we were delayed in dropping off our troops. We had a communications group that was supposed to land, but Omaha was bad. They set up their equipment on the ship and were doing on the ship what they were supposed to do on the beach."

After some time, the beach master ordered LST-511 to drop off its troops and make preparations to return to England.

"This captain in charge of the communications group went to see our captain and said, 'Look, we're doing what we're supposed to be doing here. If we go in, it's going to screw things up.' So, the skipper told him, 'I've got orders to get you guys on the beach and if you don't go and hit the beach you're going to take another ride back to England.'"

The troops pinned down on Omaha had small radios and couldn't reach their command and control groups. The communications group on 511 was already up and running and providing that vital communications link between the troops and their commands.

"The (Army) captain, having communication, got in touch with the flagship and our captain received orders to hold fast. He was doing what he was supposed to do. We held fast for two days."

At one point, he said, they were told to back off the beach even more because the Germans were shelling them. "The destroyers were going parallel with the beach trying to hit the pill boxes," he said.

McCracken said he didn't get up on deck that much, being in the engine room most of the time. However, he did say that being only a quarter-mile offshore, when he was on deck; he witnessed the confusion and carnage of the fierce fighting taking place on Bloody Omaha.

After LST-511 discharged the communications group and cargo on D+2, McCracken and the ship headed back to England.

"We were also a hospital ship. We had two Navy doctors and more than 20 corpsmen aboard," he said. "Casualties would come aboard and we'd take care of them while taking them back to England. That went on for three or four months after D-Day until airfields were built in France.

"We didn't carry any of the deceased. They were buried in France. The cemeteries in Normandy are filled with crosses."

McCracken and LST-511 went on to cross the English Channel more than 100 times in the weeks and months after D-Day delivering much needed cargo and supplies for the drive across France and into Germany.

McCracken was discharged in 1946, but participated in the decommissioning of LST-511 a year before.

"When the ship was decommissioned, nothing was mentioned about Exercise Tiger because it was still classified," he said. "I kept the secret for 40 years."

Although Tiger had remained classified, bits and pieces of information floated for decades. However, there was no complete account from official records. In the 1970s, through the Freedom of Information Act, details were released but not publicized. It would take nearly another 20 more years before McCracken knew he could talk about Exercise Tiger.

"I saw a TV program in January 1991. I really wasn't paying much attention to it. But there was this guy walking along a beach and he picked up an American silver dollar and some shrapnel. Then they said something about landing craft. That got my attention.

"He was talking about Exercise Tiger. After all these years of secrecy and now someone's talking about it on television."

McCracken started trying to get in touch with the producers of the program to contact some of the other survivors from the ill-fated exercise but he never got a response.

"Then about two months later, I saw a reunion announcement in a local newspaper for those who were in the English Channel on LSTs," he said. He called the point of contact in the announcement, a doctor who was aboard LST-507.

From that point on, McCracken got involved in an effort to get directly in touch with survivors from LST-511. Six months after seeing the TV program about Tiger, LST-511 held its first reunion and has had one every year since.

###

Joe Engel:

I Remember Pearl Harbor

On December 7, 1941, I was attached to Patrol Squadron-12 at Ka-neohe Naval Air Station, Pearl Harbor, as a naval aviation pilot (NAP)–enlisted pilot.

My family, wife Angelina and son Joseph Jr., lived on base. When we left for church that morning, just outside the main gate, we said hello to a neighbor. He was going down to the squadron hangar to repair and paint his son's bike for Christmas. This neighbor, Dale S. Lyons, had his foot blown off when a bomb destroyed the hangar. Dale later returned to active duty and qualified as a carrier pilot with an artificial foot.

As soon as we came out of church we could see the bombing and strafing. A Marine guard at the main gate said, "You're not going to bring your family in here. Can't you see we're under attack?" I told him I had to get down to the hangar and told my wife to go to the beach until it was over. She said she'd need to get a blanket and some food and proceeded to our quarters.

On the way down to the hangar I was told to report to our armory. On arrival I was given a .30-caliber rifle, ammunition and a 1918 helmet which was in two boxes: one box held the metal helmet and the other box held the leather liner and screws. It wasn't assembled and I never got it assembled. On top of that, the .30-caliber wasn't very effective for destroying aircraft.

The first attack was about 7:50 a.m. The second attack came about 25 minutes after the completion of the first attack. All our hangars were destroyed or damaged. After the attack we were told to go to the mess hall and put our white uniforms in the coffee urn to dye them so they wouldn't be so conspicuous from the air.

We salvaged machine guns from damaged PBYs and spares from the armory and set up a defense on the hill. When darkness fell, you could hear sporadic machine gun fire.

Later that evening a list of names, including mine, was called. We were told to get some sleep. We were to be bused to Pearl Harbor the next morning for patrol duty. My thoughts before going to sleep were we have our Navy and Army Air Force at Pearl and we would respond to the Japanese attack in short order. Unfortunately, I didn't know the status of these units.

I couldn't believe what I saw when I arrived at the fleet landing. It appeared that everything was on fire, ships were upside down, motor boats and motor launches were floating aimlessly with nobody in them, and oil was about 3 feet thick on the water. It was mass confusion. That night we slept on cots under the wings of PBYs that were being repaired. The noise made sleep difficult.

The next morning we took off on a 14-hour patrol. They patched the holes in the PBY hull to keep it from sinking but they missed some on top. That produced an annoying noise for 14 hours.

The floats wouldn't retract so we went on patrol with them down. That slowed us down considerably. As it turned out, the reason the floats wouldn't retract was because there was a bullet hole in some of the gear.

On that patrol we spotted, what we thought was a submarine, and dropped a depth charge on it. The submarine turned out to be a whale. That happened so often that after a while we formed a Whale Banger's Club.

On our return to the base we had no radio aids to navigate and minimal light to guide by. So when we approached Pearl Harbor, confused American gunners fired on us. On December 8, my wife and son attended the funerals of the squadron personnel killed the day before. Patrol Squadon-11 lost seven, Patrol Squadron-12 lost nine and Patrol Squadron-14 lost one. The air station lost one military member and one civilian. Ninety-seven others were wounded.

One Japanese aircraft crashed on base. The pilot, a Lt. Iida, was killed. He had apparently been the flight leader. He was buried in an adjacent grave with others that were killed. John William Finn, an aviation chief ordanceman, was awarded the Medal of Honor for heroic services and a Purple Heart for being wounded that day.

I didn't return to Pearl nor have communication with my family for three weeks. When I did return I promptly put in for air transportation back to the states for my family. Our South Sea island was no longer an island paradise.

Our living conditions at Pearl Harbor changed considerably. We had to paint the windows black, and turn out the lights before opening doors. We had fictitious air raid sirens causing families to go to the air raid shelter. Car headlights were painted black expect for a small section about the size of a silver dollar.

I still remember that our son's first words were... "Air raid, mommy!"

###

Richard Harrison:
From Omaha Beach to Paris Fireworks

For Richard Harrison, a young farmer from Coffee Springs, Alabama, World War II was a financial windfall. Harrison, like many young people during the Depression, was having a hard time finding a job, let alone one that paid decently.

"One old boy offered me 12 dollars a month to help him on his farm. I told him 'Uncle Sam will give me 21,'" says Harrison with a laugh.

Harrison's plan was simple. "They passed a law that (men) under a certain age had to have a year of military service, so I went and enlisted to get it over with. I enlisted for one year, and I was supposed to have gotten out in January 1942, but the Japanese bombed Pearl Harbor in December 1941.

"Well, that put me in there for the duration plus six (months). No getting out in January.

The day Pearl Harbor was attacked we were sitting around listening to radios and the announcer blurted out that Pearl Harbor had been bombed. They fell us out right quick and took three or four trucks to the ammunition dump, got ammunition, and came back. We loaded machine gun belts the whole Sunday afternoon. Of course, it was a few years before we got into the fighting," says Harrison, who was stationed at Fort Dix, New Jersey, at the time.

Little did Harrison know that when he did get into the fighting he would be a part of the biggest amphibious assault in history—the Normandy invasion. Harrison, a sergeant in the 4th Division engineers, made the trip across the Atlantic in a convoy of more than 300 ships. "When we were going over there, every night they'd have training. They'd fire one of those big guns and every ship in that convoy would start firing. It was just like the Fourth of July with all that fire power lighting up the sky."

Weather delayed their plans, leaving Harrison's division in southern England for a few days before the invasion. Even though they had yet to see any "action," the death toll in Harrison's division was underway.

"We had one sergeant who made out like he was the roughest, toughest thing in the 4th Division. But while we were on the ship he drank a bottle of iodine to keep from making the invasion. I don't know if he died or not. Before we got on the ship, another boy took a gun, tied the trigger to his bunk and put the barrel up (against his stomach), and while we were eating breakfast, he blew his whole inside out. It beat anything I'd ever seen," Harrison says, shaking his head. While Harrison admits that although he "dreaded" the invasion, he found resolve in his faith— in both God and the odds.

"I just decided I had just as good a chance as any of them of getting back. I wasn't going to kill myself. I had a good feeling I was coming back. I knew I had a momma and a daddy praying for me, and I could feel it."

His parents' prayers' apparently paid off. Although he and his division were part of the invasion of Omaha Beach, one of the bloodiest battle sites in American history, they were in the fifth wave of troops to hit the beach, which saw relatively few casualties. However, prayers were not enough to keep Harrison completely out of harm's way.

After the invasion, Harrison's division continued to make its way through France, preparing roads for tanks and troops. During one mine-clearing operation, Harrison was wounded. "It was early in the morning, and I felt something hit my leg. It hurt a little, but not enough to stop me right then. Well, getting on late that evening, my leg got sore," says Harrison. By the time he brought the problem to a medic, he could barely move his foot.

"I took my legging off, and there was a little hole. Then I took my boot off, and there was little hole in it, and there was a little blood and stuff in there. The medic said, 'Boy, you've got a piece of shrapnel in there. I'm going to have to send you to the collection station to have it taken out.'"

While he recovered in a Paris hospital, a visiting colonel asked Harrison if he was ready to return to his division.

41

"I told him 'Sir, going back to the 4th division would be just about like going to a division I had never seen. There weren't too many of them left when I left there.' He left, and directly a nurse came back in and said 'What kind of strings did you pull with that colonel?' I asked what she meant and she said 'He put you on limited service.'"

Limited service status meant that while Harrison would not be returned home, he would not go back to the front lines either. He requested, and received, duty at an ordnance battalion in Paris, "600 miles from the front lines. "That's where I got the letter telling me that my daddy had died. He had been dead and buried for about a month when I got the letter."

Shortly after receiving the letter, Harrison was ordered to put on his dress uniform the next morning to go see the colonel.

"I thought 'What in the world could I have done that I have to go see the colonel?'"

As it turned out, the colonel only repeated the sad news Harrison had just received, and told Harrison that since the funeral had already taken place, he would not be able to go home.

While Harrison saw the men in his squad maimed or killed by land mines, and crawled on his belly to string booby traps, all the while within earshot of the Germans, he believes the worst thing he saw was while he was out of the line of fire.

During his tour with the ordinance battalion in Paris, Harrison jumped at the opportunity to go on a train tour of part of France and Belgium. A stop along the way gave him one of his most vivid memories of the war.

"We stopped at this one place where the Germans had rounded up everyone and took them to the church house, everyone but the men. When we got there, there were just two caskets of bones, and the church had been burned down. The townspeople said when the Germans came through they rounded everyone up that couldn't go and fight, and put them in the church and then took a machine gun and mowed them down. You could see where the bullets had hit all around."

Harrison's expression goes blank, and he pauses for several seconds.

"I think the church was the worst thing I saw. I just can't imagine the Germans doing anything like that. Taking helpless children, and women, and mowing them down like that and setting the church afire."

Despite all of the carnage he saw Harrison's memories of the war range from the inhuman to the ridiculous, and eventually to the sublime.

"We took an old building that had some cases of cognac in it. Well, my corporal decided he wanted a drink, so that night he snuck back in there to get him some cognac. Well, I guess the Germans decided they wanted the same thing, but there was a whole squad of them and only one of him, so they took him prisoner. They only kept him for a few days, because we found them and took them prisoner and got him back. They didn't hurt him or anything. It made a soldier out of him, though. He never went off by himself again after that," says Harrison.

As Harrison waited out "the duration" in Paris, he was treated to a party the likes of which he had never seen. "I was in Paris when the war ended, and they celebrated for a week. There were fireworks everywhere. It was lit up like Christmas. I went up as high as they would let us go in the Eiffel Tower. They wouldn't let us go up to the very top."

Ironically, Harrison would have missed the party, but gotten home sooner if he had gone back to the 4th Division after he recovered from his wound. The division was sent stateside to prepare for fighting in the Pacific, but the war ended before they shipped out.

"I wouldn't take anything for what I know now about World War II, but Lord knows I don't want to go through it again."

###

Charles Fosha:

Not by Choice

Retired Navy Commander Charles Fosha can tell you about his World War II experiences in stunning detail. Right down to the names and ranks of most of the people he came into contact with during the war years.

Not bad, considering that by his own admission he missed most of World War II. On February 1, 1942, a month before he was supposed to receive his commission as a warrant officer, then Chief Petty Officer Fosha, a Navy enlisted pilot, was forced to make an emergency landing after an air raid on Jailut Atoll, one of the Marshall Islands in the Pacific. A master horizontal bomber, Fosha was second pilot with VT-5, a torpedo bomber squadron assigned to the USS Yorktown (CV-5).

"The weather was bad—heavy rains. I think the air raid should have been called off, but I wasn't in charge. When we got to where we knew we couldn't make it back to the carrier, my pilot said if we were lucky we might be able to get within 75 miles of it. We knew when we left we'd kind of stretching our fuel. I was told later on by some other people, that our squadron commander was against launching us that far out, but he was overruled too.

"Anyway, we knew we had to land. We couldn't possibly make it back to the carrier, so we landed on the west side of the atoll, knowing we would be captured. But you might say we had only one alternative—to proceed toward the carrier, ditch and hope we would be rescued. We decided with the weather and everything the chances of being picked up were slim to none. I found out later that two planes had gone down short of the carrier. They never found the crew from one of them, but they found a raft and it was full of bullet holes, so a Japanese ship or something probably came along and picked them off. The other plane's crew was picked up, but they were pretty close in when they ditched."

After making the tough decision to land, thereby putting their fates in the hands of the Japanese, Fosha along with the five other crew members, landed on the western side of the atoll—the Japanese were on the eastern side. The crew subsisted on rations, supplemented by coconut, breadfruit, and a chicken donated by a native of the island until they were picked up by the Japanese, two days after landing.

Their prisoner of war experience began with a plane ride to Kwajelin, where they sat, blindfolded, with their hands tied behind their backs, awaiting interrogation. In what may be a testament to Fosha's sense of humor, as well as the power of time and hindsight, Fosha is able to laugh as he recounts many of his experiences.

"We were sitting in the room on that first day, and all of the sudden we heard this "thump!" One of the boys started calling everybody's name to see if we were all still alive. This little ordnanceman with a Southern accent said 'Aw, shucks, I just fell asleep and fell over and hit my head on the floor,' but the other boy said it sounded like somebody's head had been chopped off."

During the 10 days Fosha and the rest of the crew spent on Kwajelin, they were all questioned. At one point, the 10-man board showed Fosha a Norden bombsight book marked "U.S. Navy Confidential."

"I told them that since I was enlisted, I didn't have access to classified information. I don't know if they believed me or not, but they didn't ask me about it again," says Fosha, laughing with satisfaction.

From Kwajelin the crew was put on board a Japanese steamer for Yokohoma, where they were kept in a house that had been occupied by an American Standard Oil employee and his family before the war.

"The cook for the oil company employee and his family was the same cook we had. She cooked the best creamed spinach I think I've ever eaten, and I don't particularly care for spinach."

Following his three-month stay at the house in Yokohoma, Fosha was sent to Oofuna, a new POW camp outside Yokohoma without the rest of the crew. "I was at Oofuna for 10 days by myself, and I was locked in a room the first few nights, but after that they just had me sleep in the guards' room. I had one sleeping alongside me and one sleeping up by my head. If I had to go during the night one of them would get up and go with me. After about a night of that, they just said 'go.' After all, there really weren't too many places I could run to."

When more POWs began to arrive at the camp, Fosha was moved to Zentsuji, where the rest of his crew had been sent from Yokohoma. "Later we got some people from Oofuna at Zentsuji, and they said Oofuna had gotten pretty rough," says Fosha.

Fosha and the other enlisted prisoners worked six days a week, which Fosha says helped them keep track of time. He said that being an enlisted worker had another advantage. "We got bigger food rations than the officers because we were working."

Of all the jobs he did, which included supervising terracing work and loading/unloading railroad cars, Fosha remembers his time spent working at a Japanese bakery as the most rewarding, at least in terms of calories.

"We weren't supposed to eat anything, but the electric ovens we did the baking in were hidden out of view by the steam ovens," says Fosha, Smiling. Fosha managed to supplement his meager camp rations of rice, soup and bread with enough bakery goodies to weigh in at 195 pounds by the time his tour at the bakery ended as the result of a joke that misfired.

"One of the guys had been scuffling in the barracks, and he got a little cut above his eyebrow. The next day at work he had a little bandage on it, and all the Japanese wanted to know what had happened. As a joke, he said that I hit him. Well, to the Japanese this was all right, because they knew I was senior to him. They would come by and ask about it. This went on for a few days, then the boss came out of his office and tried to make us shake hands and said 'tomodache,' that means friends. We wouldn't do it. We'd say 'Tomodache, Ni.' After about the third day of this, when I got back to the barracks the interpreter sent for me. He said 'Your attitude has not been good.' So it was back to the railroad I went."

Throughout his recollection of his POW experience, Fosha emphasizes that he never faced the brutality that other POWs encountered. This may be why he doesn't carry any animosity toward the Japanese.

"We were all caught up in world events, and although they were wrong to bomb Pearl Harbor," wrote Fosha in a recollection of his POW experience for the Silver Eagle Association, a group of former enlisted aviators, "we all basically followed the dictates of our leaders."

But Fosha doesn't share in the post World War II nostalgia that has swept America, either. "Of course, you could say I missed most of the war," says Fosha, laughing. "I don't figure I have any nostalgia about World War II. I remember being a prisoner of war, but it doesn't keep me awake at night. I've accepted it. I guess I always did. You just accept what happened and move on."

Fosha pauses for a moment, and his expression saddens. "I got mail from the wife about once a month, and they let us write a letter about once a month... about 40 or 50 words. You really couldn't say much, except that you were still alive," Fosha says, his voice beginning to quiver and his eyes watering. Fosha's first child was born while he was a POW.

"My wife told me just before the war that she was pregnant. I was captured in February and our son was born in August."

Charles Fosha Jr. was three years old when he met his father for the first time in October 1945.

"When I first went into the camp at Zentsuji, the Japanese were making recordings, and the senior American officer said 'If your family doesn't know that you're a POW, go ahead and make the recording.'"

All you could do was identify yourself, and say 'I'm in the prison camp and notify so-and-so.

"My wife got something like 80 or 90 cards or letters from different people, because the Japanese were broadcasting it on shortwave radio. Tokyo Rose might have been the one doing the broadcasting; I don't know. A minister sent my wife a record of the broadcast, with words of comfort on the other side."

Fosha's wife, Edna, received official word that her husband was a POW in late July 1944, almost six months after he was taken captive, and about a week before she gave birth to Charles Jr. Despite the hardships he and his family faced during his POW experience, Fosha has managed to find a bright side to an otherwise dismal time in his life.

"Knowing what I know now, I think if I hadn't been captured I probably would have been at the Battle of Midway, the battle where we lost the most torpedo planes. I think that out of a whole squadron of torpedo planes, we lost all but one. So who knows? I might have been killed at Midway," says Fosha who retired from the Navy in 1969.

###

Albert Duke:

Remembering the Queen of the Flattops

You're 17 years old. You've been in the Navy about four months. You're at your battle station, far below deck in the after boiler room.

Suddenly the entire ship shudders. The muffled sound of an explosion reverberates throughout the ship.

"Torpedo!" someone, shouts. You desperately try to recall what they told you in boot camp. What if the ship goes down? What if the compartment is filled with smoke? What if you're trapped below decks? What if...?

If you're Albert Clifford Duke you rely on the wisdom of your chief and your own survival instincts.

In May 1942, Duke was a 17-year fireman aboard the USS Lexington (CV-2) when the carrier—dubbed "Queen of the Flat Tops" by war correspondent Stanley Johnston—was sunk during the Battle of the Coral Sea.

"I was fresh out of boot camp (recruit training), when I reported aboard the Lexington at Pearl Harbor," Duke recalls. "I was assigned to the B Division and put to work in the air compressor room in the after boiler room. That was also my battle station during general quarters (GQ). Man, it was hot down there," Duke says, with a wiping motion of his brow.

"That's why I became an Airedale (airman). I couldn't wait to get out of that hole. The only 'cool' air we got down there was from big vents. And the air coming out of those things was around 100 degrees."

Duke barely had enough time to become acquainted with his workspace when the 15-year-old aircraft carrier put to sea. She soon joined with the USS Yorktown (CV-5) to intercept an enemy troop transport and carrier force moving into the Coral Sea.

The young man from the Florida Panhandle was about to get his first bitter taste of combat. "I had just gotten off watch and went topside to get a breath of fresh air," Duke says. "I guess I had been up there about 10 minutes, when GQ was sounded. I went back below to my battle station. About two minutes later the first torpedoes hit.

"The ship shook, the lights went out and smoke from the fires topside started filtering through the vents into the compressor room. The other guys at my GQ station, I believe there were 13... maybe 14 of us, started coughing, wheezing and wiping their eyes. I was a little luckier than some of them because I had a gas mask.

"For some reason," Duke pauses, trying to recall the exact chain of events, "after I had gotten off watch, I stopped by my berthing compartment for something or the other, and on the way topside I grabbed the mask hanging, on the end of my bunk, and attached it to my belt.

"All the guys had been issued gas masks," he says sorrowfully. But they were always getting in the way, so we didn't always keep them with us.

"Anyway," he continues, "a few minutes later the ship shook again, pretty soon, the entire boiler room was filling up with smoke and steam. By this time I was beginning to get a little concerned. "Now you got to understand," Duke says, "we were way below decks. We had no way of knowing what was actually happening topside, except what little information we could get from the phone talker on the bridge. We could hear bombs exploding and every now and then we would be knocked off our feet. Still, we tried our best to keep the compressors going. That was our job."

A couple of hours after the first torpedo hit, according to Duke, the Lexington began to list. Fires, caused by gasoline and ignited by exploding bombs, were burning out of control throughout the ship. After more than three hours of battling the flames, it became apparent that the Lexington was going to be lost.

"We heard Capt. (Frederick) Sherman give the order to abandon ship, but when we tried to get out, the hatch, which must have been warped by the heat, wouldn't open...we were trapped. There was nothing we could do. We couldn't get out and the damage control parties couldn't get to us to force the hatch open because of the smoke and fire in the hangar deck.

"The chief, Chief Sutton, I never did know his first name. We just called him Chief Sutt. Anyway, the chief said, 'boys we're on our own. We'll have to get out the best way we can. You boys with gas masks, put 'em on. The rest of you try to find a cloth, wet it, and put it over your mouth and nose. Line up and hold on to the man in front of you. I'll take the lead. We'll try to make it out through the scuttle.'"

Duke says he knew that if there was anyone in the air compressor room who could get them out it would be the chief.

"He was a little man, 'bout 5-feet tall. He had been aboard Lexington for 13 years and knew the engineering spaces like the back of his hand. When we were all lined up and holding on to one another, the chief looked back at us and said 'alright hang on to the guy's belt in front. When I pop this scuttle scoot through as quick as you can and make your way to the weather decks.' I was hanging on to the chief for dear life. I figured that if he made it, I would too.

"By this time things were really getting bad. A steam line had parted and the decks and the chains on the ladder (used for handrails) were so hot you couldn't touch them. The guy behind me let go of my belt and that messed it up for the other guys. But let me tell you, I hung on to the chief.

"As I said it was pitch dark, and despite the fact that the chief had been on the ship all those years, he had trouble finding the hatch leading to the hangar bay. Finally, though, he found another hatch leading into the machine shop. We could hear the other guys down below screaming and shouting. "Somehow Chief Sutton got the hatch undogged and shoved me into the machine shop. 'You go ahead,' he said. 'I gotta go back and get those guys.' I said, chief, you'll never make it. 'I gotta try, 'he told me. You go on and get outta here. That was the last I ever saw of him.

"I made my way to the flight deck, and this officer handed me a Mae West (life jacket). I sat down on the deck took off my shoes and grabbed hold of a line and started sliding down into the water. But my hands were pretty badly burned, and I couldn't hold on. I let go of the line and dropped into the water. Man... I thought I was never going to come back to the surface." When he eventually reached the surface, Duke looked about for a boat or other floating objects.

"After a few minutes a life raft came floating by. Must have been 50 men on that raft, although it was designed to hold only 25. Anyway, I grabbed onto it too. By now it was getting dark. We paddled out about a hundred yards from the stern of the ship. It wasn't long after that when we were picked up by a whale boat from the cruiser Minneapolis."

After being returned to the states, Duke and his surviving shipmates were offered 30 days survivors leave. Duke says he and several other Lexington survivors turned down the leave, simply because they couldn't afford to go very far on $21 a month.

"I was sent to Sand Point Naval Air Station in Seattle Washington, to be part of a new squadron being formed up—VTF-21.

"When I got to Seattle the squadron had a total of four airplanes. I guess because there were so many men checking into the squadron, and they didn't have anything for us to do, we were formed up into a CASU (Carrier Aircraft Service Unit)—CASU-17, given some commando training and sent back to the Pacific.

When CASU-17 reached Hawaii, they were assigned to the 2nd Marine Division and put through five more weeks of commando-style training before deploying to Betlo Island, then called Island X in November 1943.

After 17 months of servicing and maintaining allied aircraft during the day and being harassed by Japanese bombers at night, Duke reported to Jacksonville, Florida, where he worked in the aircraft maintenance division until he was discharged from the Navy on December 10, 1945.

###

Ray Carlson:

Twice a Chief

Making chief petty officer in the United States Navy is an awesome task. An accomplishment most Navy people—thankfully—only have to worry about once.

But for retired Chief Petty Officer Raymond Carlson, once wasn't enough.

Carlson, a World War II veteran, was discharged from the Navy in 1946 after having advanced from seaman recruit to chief aviation machinist's mate. "I went to work for Vought Aircraft after getting out of the Navy," Carlson says, "but after a while I got bored and decided I wanted to return to the Navy."

Considering that the Bridgeport, Connecticut, native had once been listed as having gone down with the USS Lexington (CV-2) and had survived the sinking of the USS Yorktown (CV-5), it's little wonder that he found civilian life to be somewhat on the dull side. So in May 1949, former Chief Petty Officer Ray Carlson visited the nearest Navy Recruiting Office.

"I had made chief pretty fast and of course the military was a lot smaller, so I figured I might have to take a drop in grade. But I wasn't expecting to drop all the way back to petty officer second class.

"'You're lucky to be getting back in at any grade,' the recruiter told me. And you know what? He was right. Besides, I figured, what the hey! I made chief once. I can do it again.

Two months after his initial enlistment in December 1939, the 18-year-old sailor reported to Torpedo Squadron Five (VP-5) aboard the USS Yorktown (CV-5) at San Diego, California.

"I didn't have a lot of training when I reported aboard so I was given a choice of being a mess cook or doing some typing in the ship's office. I took the typing job," Carlson laughed. "Course I didn't know it at the time, but that turned out to be a smart decision. Besides, not only was the typing job better than mess cooking, I also had an opportunity to learn office and Navy personnel procedures.

While working in the ship's office, Carlson requested, and received orders for a six-month Aviation Machinist's Mate course at Norfolk, Virginia

"In those days getting about was difficult. The Yorktown was based at Pearl Harbor and the only way to get back to the states was by ship. By the time I got to Norfolk my class had already started, so I had to wait for the next class to commence.

"I had only been in school a couple of days when I had to have my tonsils removed. The doctors at Portsmouth Naval Hospital said I would be in the hospital for at least three days, so I was set back again. But, I finally made it through school and graduated in February 1942.

One of my classmates, a fellow by the name of Earl Simmons, had orders to my squadron aboard the Yorktown. I was assigned to his old division, the V-2 Division, aboard the Lexington.

While in transit back to Pearl Harbor aboard a transport, we tried to get our orders swapped. But we were told that we would have to wait until we got to the receiving unit at Pearl. When we reached Pearl, we were again given the run-around. 'You'll have to wait until you get to CASU-5 (Carrier Aircraft Service Unit). They have your records,' we were told.

"When we checked into CASU-5 the first thing Simmons and I did was go see the jg (lieutenant junior grade). 'Can't help you,' he told us. 'You'll have to go over to the flag office and get the admiral to change the orders.' So off we go to the flag office were we reported to a Lieutenant Commander Rawlings.

"Sir," I told Mr. Rawlings, Simmons and I are assigned to each other's ship. He wants to get back to the Lexington and I want to get back aboard the Yorktown.'"

'You're both third class,' Rawlings said, 'shouldn't be a problem. Yeoman, take care of it,' he said, to his yeoman.

"We thanked Mr. Rawlings and happily went on our way. Simmons back to the Lexington—which was in port at the time—and me back to the CASU to wait for the Yorktown."

As far as Carlson and Simmons were concerned everything was under control. Under control that is until payday rolled around. After standing in the pay line for nearly an hour, Carlson sadly discovered his name wasn't on the pay list.

"Whatta you mean my name's not on the pay list?' I asked."

'Sorry. We don't have your records. Without a pay record we can't pay you,' the pay master told me."

Putting two and two together, Carlson figured that although his orders to the Lexington had been changed, his records had somehow been forwarded on to Lexington. Now the problem was to try and retrieve them.

I was in charge of a working party that day and ironically, we were supposed to take a load of mail to the Lexington. When we got to the ship the first person I saw was Simmons, standing at the head of the gangway. I explained my problem to Simmons and he took me to see the V-2 Division chief.

'Carlson! Where the hell have you been,' the chief bellowed. 'You're AOL.'

"After explaining how the mix-up had occurred, I asked the chief if I could get my records...at least my pay record.

'Can't do it,' the chief says. 'You gotta have something in writing. How do I know you are who you say you are?'

Feeling dejected, Carlson returned to the CASU and explained the problem to the duty officer. This is where Carlson's earlier office experience paid off. Assisting the duty officer and yeoman, he acquired the necessary paperwork and returned to the Lexington. In his excitement of the prospect of finally getting paid, he forgot to go to sick bay to retrieve his medical record.

A day or so later, Lexington put to sea where she joined up with Yorktown for the Battle of the Coral Sea. In the meantime, Carlson is still in Hawaii waiting for Yorktown. When the Yorktown finally arrived Carlson was filled with excitement. Finally he was going to be reunited with his old shipmates.

"I didn't know a soul when I went back aboard," Carlson remembers" All my friends were gone. Worse yet, they really didn't have a job for me so I was assigned to the propeller shop."

After a few days in the yards to repair damage suffered during the Battle of the Coral Sea, Yorktown returned to sea. In the meantime, back in Bridgeport, Petty Officer Carlson's family was being notified that he had gone down with the Lexington. "They had recovered my medical record from the debris, and of course the Navy assumed that I was aboard the Lexington when she went down."

"I was in the propeller shop all by myself when suddenly, BOOM! BOOM! BOOM! I hear the five-inchers firing. I went outside onto a platform deck. Looking toward the horizon I see four small specks. I don't know if they are theirs or ours. Then came the boop-boop-boop-boop! of the one point ones. The specks grew larger and all of a sudden—KABOOM! KABOOM! KABOOM! Three, maybe four, bombs hit the ship. Like a fool, I'm still standing out there trying to see what's going on. I wasn't scared... just inquisitive.

The attack put us out of commission for a few minutes. But we got the boilers back on line and had the speed up to about 18 knots when Japanese torpedo planes hit us. I'm still standing out on that platform. I hear an explosion and I'm knocked on my fanny. I got up, and I was knocked down again. Torpedoes had hit on the port side. I was on the starboard so I didn't realize what had happened.

"The ship began to list and I remember thinking... 'Gee the captain is really turning this thing on its side.' Then we went dead in the water. People were running around, shouting and attempting to lower lifeboats and rafts when the word was passed to abandon ship. Because of the list, we were told to take our shoes off. It was easier to move around without them. Well I took off my shoes and neatly laid them across an aircraft chock, figuring I would come back and get them later," Carlson chuckled.

Carlson said a chief then told him to go aft and wait. When the word was given to abandon ship Carlson slid down a line into the water and was later picked up by the destroyer Hammon. "Our executive officer was also picked up by the Hammon and told us a story about his steward. Seems the XO wasn't quite ready to leave Yorktown but the steward was. So when the XO told him he was ready to leave the steward reportedly asked, 'Sir, would be all right if I went ahead and waited for you in water, Sir?'"

After being rescued, Carlson was assigned to a torpedo bomber squadron aboard the Enterprise (CV-6). On August 24, 1942, Carlson was on the flight deck, aft of the island, awaiting the return of his aircraft, when the Enterprise came under attack.

"After the Yorktown, I had no desire to lollygag topside. A bomb hit the number two elevator and a fellow in a gun tub just above me had his foot just about blown off. Four of us got a hold of him and took him below to sickbay. We were on our way back topside when a second bomb hit the five-inch gun galley on the starboard side-killing everyone in the galley."

Having survived major battles in the Pacific aboard the Yorktown and Enterprise, Carlson was assigned to the USS Saratoga (CV-3) where he remained until March 1944. Carlson made chief in 1945 and left the Navy in 1946.

After reenlisting in the Navy, Carlson continued to advance until he made chief for a second time in 1962. He retired from the Navy in August 1968.

###

Betty Cain:

War Bride

No story of World War II would be complete without at least a mention of the "war brides." One of those ladies who married an American serviceman during the war is Perth, Australia, native Betty Cain.

Cain was serving in the Women's Australian Air Force when she met her future husband, Charles E. Cain, an American sailor serving in Australia. She immigrated to the United States in 1944, after she and Charles were married. She became an American citizen in 1952.

"I was working as a telephone operator when the war actually broke out," the youthful World War II veteran says, laughing. "I also remember that I had the mumps and walked around with a big bandage tied around my jaw.

"At that time, everyone who wasn't working in an essential service was subject to the draft. Telephone operators were considered essential so I didn't have to go in the service, but my older sister talked me into joining the Air Force with her. 'We'll always be together,' she told me. Well, that lasted until we finished boot camp. My sister entered the officer corps but I couldn't because you had to be at least 21 to go to officer's training school and I was only 18. So much for staying together," she laughed.

After basic military training and some technical training where she learned how to identify and plot aircraft, Betty was assigned to an American Navy PBY base which had previously been the University of West Australia.

"The base was on Crawley Bay, which was only about four miles from home. I spent all my Air Force service at that base," she adds. "We had a tennis court at our house and my mom let the Americans use the court during the weekdays. But my dad, who was a union official and had to approve all travel outside of Perth, put his foot down when it came to dating the Yanks. He was absolutely opposed to it."

Recalling her Air Force days, Cain who still speaks with a slight Australian accent, said that despite the fact that it has been more than 60 years, she can still recall being attacked by magpies each time she would leave her building.

"The only thing I can figure is that for some reason the birds didn't like our uniforms," she laughs. "We (Air Force women) were the only ones they bothered. Anyone wearing khaki or white could come and go without any problem. But as soon as one of our girls stepped out of the building in our blue uniforms, the birds would swoop down on us. Strangely enough, if someone escorted us in khaki, the birds wouldn't bother us.

"The Americans had a photo lab on the second floor of the building that I worked in and at noon we would all gather outside to eat lunch so I got to know the Yanks pretty well. I used to make it a point to have one of the chiefs in the photo lab escort me each time I left the building.

"I suppose you could say it was because of the birds that I met my husband," Cain chuckled.

"If he hadn't been visiting the photo lab," she continued, "we would probably have never met. One Friday night he asked me out and the very next Friday he asked me to marry him."

"I must admit, that took me back a bit. 'Wow!' I remember saying, 'I heard you Yanks were fast, but not this fast.'"

The quickness of Cain's proposal notwithstanding, Betty Accepted the American's marriage proposal then spent the next several weeks trying to get through the necessary procedures of requesting permission to marry.

"There were so many Americans getting married that the Navy required a six-month waiting period. I also had to have official permission, so the mayor—a family friend—signed for me and as soon as I turned 21 we got married. My parents weren't too happy about it though. I don't think my father ever totally forgave me. Oh, they liked Charles alright, they just didn't want me to marry him," Cain confesses.

While waiting for the six-month waiting period to pass, Betty was released from service, thus overcoming one obstacle to eventually immigrating to the United States. In September 1944, Charles received orders back to the states and wanted Betty to join him in Sydney for the trip home. Though it was seemingly a simple request, the young couple discovered there was a rough road ahead. To begin with, travel from one part of Australia to another was nearly impossible without the approval of none other than Betty's father and he was in no mood to grant permission for his daughter to leave home— possibly to never be seen again.

"At the time dad was out of town on official business," Betty recalls, "so I called his secretary and told her that I needed to get to Sydney and dad had said it was OK. She signed the waiver for me to go. She nearly lost her job over it, but I had my travel permit," she smiles.

Although many war brides had to travel to the states by themselves, Betty and Charles were able to travel on the same ship but were berthed in different sections of the ship.

"We were allowed to be together only one hour a day."

Her father's concern about not seeing his daughter again proved to be true. Her first visit back to her homeland was in 1968—24 years after she bid her family and friends farewell and sailed to America as a "war bride."

###

Simon J. Burttschell II:

<u>Natural Born Pilot</u>

World War II affected many people in many different ways. From families who lost loved ones, to Soldiers, Sailors, Marines and Airmen who witnessed unspeakable traumas, to those at home who prayed for their safety, listening to tunes written for the boys over there and seemingly ever-present propaganda.

Almost every American had an active role in the war. Whether they were in the trenches or in their kitchens, saving metal for the effort, or working in a factory for the cause, every moment of life revolved around what was happening in Europe and the Pacific.

Retired Navy Commander Simon J. Burttschell II is one of those Americans who chose to take the front line route. Although he was fortunate never to have engaged in combat, World War II affected him for the rest of his life. Ask him why he wanted to fly, and he will tell you this, "I was a young man, 6 or 7 years old. My grandfather owned a Chevrolet agency and he had a mechanic that was a World War I fighter pilot named Thurman West. Thurman had sent back some pieces of German aircraft from over there, and got some other surplus aircraft parts, and he and my grandfather put it together in his garage.

Thurman finally got the engine working and got it airborne. One day he was flying it and I was out watching him. All of a sudden I saw him spinning straight down over the river. I ran screaming to my mother and I told her Thurman had crashed!"

West hadn't crashed but was only testing the plane's maneuverability. That experience so thrilled Burttschell that from that day on his fascination with airplanes and flying grew. "That made me want to fly, and I just kept at it."

World War II began while Burttschell was in college. He desperately wanted to fly, so he phoned his father to request permission. After his father's refusal, Burttschell was urged by then Texas Congressman Lyndon Johnson, whom Burttschell's father had called, to stay in school because... "After the war we'll need some smart people in this country," the future president of the United States, told Burttschell.

Burttschell was disappointed to no end. He convinced his father to enroll him at Texas A&M, which was an Army military college with a "top notch ROTC program," according to Burttschell. When the aspiring pilot turned 18, he and six of his classmates went to Dallas, Texas, to the Army Air Corps recruiting office."

"There was an old red-headed major sitting there reading the newspaper, and he had his lunch out. And he says, "What do you boys want?" I was leading the bunch. So I said we want to join up in the Army Air Corps."

"And he said, 'Well, I can't help you right now, its lunchtime.' That disappointed me. I thought they would just reach out and grab us, you know? Be happy to get us. I was real disappointed. But that didn't stop us from pursuing their dreams. We walked around the corner to a Navy recruiter's office—they were happy to get us."

After three months of ground school training at a junior college, Burttschell finally became airborne via CPT; Civilian Pilot Training. His instructor put him through the ringer during his first flight, and Burttschell passed with more than flying colors.

"He put the plane into a spin and I watched the way he was doing it with the controls and all. He took it up again, after he recovered, and put it in another spin. He said OK, you got it, now recover! Which I did."

His first flight in an airplane, and he recovered perfectly. The instructor made the note 'natural born pilot' in Burttschell's logbook after that first flight.

Later in his career, when Burttschell began instructing, he used his first flight as a lesson. "See, if a guy was scared to death, I didn't think he'd make it (as a pilot)."

Burttschell felt very relaxed in airplanes. "I always felt that I wore an airplane, or that it wore me, I just fit right in there—it wasn't strange or anything—you know?"

After receiving his wings, the new pilot was sent to Melbourne, Florida, for F6F Hellcat fighter training. "I loved that plane," remarked Burttschell.

One afternoon in Melbourne, 250 aspiring pilots lined up on the flight line. Shoulder to shoulder, they listened to a visiting captain extol the virtues of night fighter flying, and what it took to become a night pilot. After about a five-minute speech, he said "All those who want to be a night fighter, hold up your hands."

Burttschell immediately thrust his hand up in the air, punctuating his still evident exuberance. But back then, on the flight line, the fearless young pilot was the only one with his hand in the air.

Obviously, this wasn't the reaction the captain was looking for. He hurriedly counted off 25 of the pilots, including Burttschell, and designated them as candidates for night training. Two hours later, the men were packed and on their way to their new school.

After training, Burttschell reported to the carrier USS Saratoga. The carrier was going to dry dock, so Burttschell and his squadron VF (n) -52, awaited the USS Bonhomme Richard (CV-31).

While waiting at Pearl Harbor, Burttschell recalls listening to the radio. "The thing that really tickled us... Tokyo Rose came on the air and called out my name and a bunch of other names in our squadron and said 'Come on out boys. Our boys are waiting to shoot you down.'

"Everybody laughed," he said. "We thought it was a big joke—we just couldn't wait to get out there and shoot them down."

Burttschell never had an opportunity to fight his radio enemies. "We were one of the first night air groups to go aboard a carrier," he says. "We didn't do any day work at all.

"We were part of a task force, and we were supposed to protect the carrier at night from any invading Japanese aircraft." Burttschell's squadron would fly NACP (night air carrier patrol). While one pilot was up in the air, the next would be waiting on the catapult. "It was an all-night vigil, but there were no Japanese aircraft left by then."

Burttschell was a bit disappointed by the lack of action. "You train a football player to play football, that's all he wants to do," he says. "So when you're trained to shoot down enemy planes, you want to shoot them down."

Burttschell, once one of the shining aviators of the Navy, served his country with valor, strength and a no fear attitude that led him through the Navy's test pilot and missile launch programs, and eventually on to NASA. He was indeed a natural born pilot.

###

Bill Pugh:

Flying Boat Pilot recalls final flight

The role of naval aviation in World War II, particularly in the Pacific, is a Well documented fact. The daring escapades of naval aviators such as David McCampbell— the Navy's first World War II ace—Gregory "Pappy" Boyington, Elbert McCuskey and Joseph Foss are legendary. But for every ace, flying the hottest aircraft of the period, there were thousands of others flying a variety of aircraft, who played an equally important role. Men such as retired Navy Chief Petty Officer Bill Pugh.

When the Sedalia, Missouri, native graduated from high school in May 1934 the nation was in the midst of a depression.

Employment was only something the graduating seniors had read about during their school days. Jobs for teenagers were completely out of the question.

"I knew I wasn't going to find work in Sedalia, so I and a buddy of mine decided we would go down and join the Navy."

When Pugh and his high school buddy arrived at the recruiting station, they quickly discovered that joining the Navy would probably be easier said than done. Thirty-four other Sedalia youths, many of them former high school classmates, took the initial armed forces entrance exam that day. Only two—Pugh and his buddy passed.

"We were put on a bus and sent on to the main recruiting station in St. Louis," Pugh recalls. "I was accepted into the Navy, but they sent my buddy home. 'Too much of an overbite of his upper teeth,' they said."

After completing recruit training at San Diego, Pugh reported to the USS Lexington (CV-2).

After two years of working as a deck seaman in the First Division, and after repeated requests for transfer, he was finally reassigned to VF-1B, the Lexington fighter squadron.

"Upon returning from a Hawaiian cruise in 1937, VF-1B was transferred to Norfolk, Virginia, and combined with VF-6, the Enterprise squadron. I joined the Navy with the intention of only staying in for four years. My plan was to save enough money to go to college. But somewhere along the way I decided that I wanted to fly. I applied for flight school and was told that I would be called when a class date was available.

"As it happened, by the time my enlistment was up I still hadn't been called, so I got out and went to Seattle, Washington, where I took a job with Boeing Aircraft."

After four years in the Navy, Pugh soon become bored building aircraft and decided to go talk with the Navy recruiter about reenlisting.

"With war brewing in Europe, it wasn't difficult this time," Pugh said. "Recruiters were welcoming people, especially veterans, with open arms. "I'm willing to reenlist, I told the recruiter, if I can go to flight school.

"The recruiter said he would send in my request and get back in touch with me. I went ahead and reenlisted and it wasn't long after that, maybe a week or so that I got a letter telling me that I would be accepted for flight training upon passing the flight physical. Regrettably, I failed part of the eye exam and was turned down.

"I was eligible for shore duty, so I asked for duty in Pensacola, Florida. I still wasn't convinced that I had problems with my eyes, so the first thing that I did when reporting for duty at Corry Field at Pensacola, was to go to sick bay and have my eyes re-examined. Sure enough, I passed."

Pugh's jubilation was short lived, however. Because he had failed the first exam, and turned down for flight training, he had to retake the entire flight physical over again. The repeat exam confirmed that he did indeed have a slight problem with his eyes again disqualifying him for flight training. Disappointed, Pugh all but gave up his dream of flying and returned to his duties as an aviation machinist's mate at Corry Field.

Gradually he advanced in rate to first class petty officer, got married and transferred to a PBY squadron at the Pensacola Naval Air Station.

"One day, I was passing by a bulletin board and noticed a request for flight training volunteers. The date was December 13, 1941. World War II was a week old. At first, I had some reservations. I was now married and had two daughters. But my desire to fly won out and this time I was accepted for flight training and was awarded my Navy Wings of Gold in June 1942.

Believing that he would be receiving some additional training once he arrived at his new duty station near San Francisco, Pugh and his wife, Ruth, gave up their apartment, sold their furniture and bought one of the last new cars available in Pensacola—a 1942 Studebaker—loaded up the kids and his sister-in-law, and headed west.

Three days after arriving in San Francisco, Pugh was en route to Kaneohe Bay, Hawaii, for duty as an enlisted pilot assigned to Patrol Squadron-91 (VP-91). In the meantime, his wife, back in San Francisco, sold the Studebaker and returned to Pensacola.

"Patrol Squadron-91 arrived in the southwestern Pacific in October 1942. We were based at Esperitu Santos in the New Hebrides Islands and operating from the seaplane tenders USS Curriss and Mackinac. Our primary job was to try and find the Japanese fleet."

VP-91, according to Pugh, was a 12-plane PBY Catalina flying boat squadron. Each PBY flew individual sector searches covering approximately 800 miles out and back from the base ship. Each PBY carried 1,760 gallons of fuel and four 500-pound combination surface bombs or depth charges. On October 11, 1942, five of the planes were sent north to Vanikoro Island for a four-day advanced patrol.

"Our mission was to search for the Japanese fleet steaming south to deliver a knockout blow to our forces on Guadalcanal. The first two days were uneventful. But on the third day we lost one plane to Japanese carrier fighter planes. My plane picked up the only radio report from the downed PBY. The brief report said the PBY was being attacked by Zeroes. That was the last we heard from them. On the third day of the patrol, we ran upon a Zero. We surely couldn't take the Zero on in a dogfight, so we dropped our depth charges and ducked into a cloudbank to evade the Japanese fighter. Well, when we came out of the clouds, right there, below us, was the entire Japanese fleet, except for carriers. We hung around on the edge of the fleet, just out of range of their antiaircraft fire, and relayed their position back to the base.

"On the fourth and last day of the mission we lost a second plane — presumably to Zeroes. About this same time, my plane located a Japanese carrier. We barely managed to get off our position report before two Zeroes were after us. I can't say for certain, but I think their first pass hit our gas tank. At any rate, we were on fire and heading for the water 6,000 feet below."

"At the time of the attack Lieutenant Gordon B. Snyder was the aircraft commander. I was in the nose section of the plane. Policy at the time dictated that when the aircraft was engaged in combat operations, the enlisted pilot would man the .30-caliber machine gun in the nose of the PBY.

"Thinking that the plane would make a crash landing on the water, I elected to remain in the nose position rather than go back in the fuselage where the survival gear was located... a decision which probably saved my life.

"As we neared the water I was thinking that it should be about time to start leveling off. Then suddenly, WHAM! Under we went— without even a bounce. The forward hull was ripped open by the impact, and the inrush of water, forced me out through a small opening at the top of a gun turret. By the time I reached the surface of the water, flames from the gas and oil fire had been pushed behind me by the wind and swells."

"My right shoulder was out of place and lower right leg had a compound fracture. As a result of the wounds, I was struggling to stay afloat when I saw a seabag floating nearby and grabbed it."

"The seabag was a godsend, but after a while it became waterlogged and was no longer useful as a float. Scanning the area for something else to hang on to, I spotted one of the wing-tip floats from the PBY floating about 50 feet away. Swimming was nearly impossible because of my wounds, but I did manage to dog paddle to the float and grab on. It wasn't long after that when a PBY from another search sector appeared on the horizon.

The plane was from a detachment of Pugh's squadron, assigned to Esperitu Santos. Normally, according to Pugh, the detachment's search sectors were about 150 to 200 miles apart, but for some reason this plane just happened to be about 70 miles to the rear when it picked up the radio reports from Pugh's plane.

Seeing the trail of smoke from Pugh's PBY, the pilot of the Esperitu Santos PBY headed for the area. Exiting a cloudbank he had been using as cover, the pilot, Lieutenant Richard J. Teich, saw Pugh, hanging onto the wing tip float. He made a low pass and dropped two rubber rafts. Because of the wind and sea state the rafts landed far beyond the immediate area.

"I thought they might have to leave me in the water until a ship could arrive," Pugh said, "but a minute or so later, I noticed the pilot setting up for an open sea landing."

Upon arrival at Esperitu Santos, Pugh learned that he was the sole survivor of the three planes lost. Each plane carried a crew of eight.

Chief Pugh said that while he owes a great deal to the PBY crew that picked him up, he believes that a higher authority orchestrated his rescue.

"I attribute my rescue not only to my own prayers to the Almighty, but to those of my loved ones, as well."

After several months in a hospital at San Francisco recovering from his injuries, Chief Pugh requested to be transferred back to Pensacola.

"After about six weeks the request came back approved, providing I was willing to pay my own train fare," Pugh laughed.

As a result of his wartime injuries and bones which never healed properly, Chief Pugh never flew again as a pilot.

###

Dean Axene:

Undersea Warrior

From its inception, the submarine service has been commonly referred to as the "silent service." Sailors who put to sea in these small, cramped submergible craft during World War II depended on stealth and the depths of the oceans to carry out their deadly mission — Missions from which 52 American submarines never returned from patrol during World War II. This loss represented a casualty rate of nearly 22 percent — the highest casualty rate for any branch of the U.S. military. Despite the high casualty rate, or perhaps because of it, few branches of the military have been more romanticized in movies and books than the men of the silent service.

Retired Rear Admiral Dean Axene, is one of those undersea warriors. Though it was late in the war before the admiral made his first war patrol, it didn't lessen the danger or the thrill of engaging the enemy from beneath the seas.

"I graduated from the Naval Academy in June 1944, and after Submarine School at New London, Connecticut, arrived in the Pacific in the spring of 1945," Axene said.

"I was young and patriotic not yet 22 — but I was anxious to help win the war. My first assignment was to a relief crew at Pearl Harbor where I became involved in the refitting of the submarine USS Parche (SS-384). At the end of the refit, I was ordered aboard as the assistant gunnery officer. At the time I didn't think it could get much better. Here I was a junior officer in a modern fleet type submarine—carrying the war to the very doorstep of the enemy. Like I said, I was very young—and very naive," the admiral said, smiling.

Axene made two war patrols aboard the Parche and despite the fact that the war was nearly over, day-to-day operations were still very real. So much so that as a result of the first patrol, the Parche's skipper, Commander Woodrow Wilson McCrory, was awarded the Navy Cross and Axene was awarded the Bronze Star.

"Both patrols were made in coastal waters on the east side of Honshu, ranging from the Tsugaru Straits on the north, southward to roughly the parallel at which Sendai, Japan is located," Axene recalls. "Japan's maritime forces had been pretty heavily mauled by mid-1945 and targets were scarce. We had to scratch for targets, and we did —with considerable success, I might add." Because Parche's patrol area was in Japanese waters, enemy help from home was always close at hand and every encounter involved threat and risk for Parche and her crew.

"This situation led to some close calls," Axene remembers. "Two in particular, seemed especially close to me and one of these involved a depth charge attack which nearly did us in.

"One day we made a daylight, submerged torpedo attack on a small, escorted coastal convoy. As I recall, the escort was comprised of two small destroyer-type ships and sporadic air cover from nearby Honshu. Our attack on the main body of the convoy was successful resulting in extensive damage to at least one of the merchant ships. However, the destroyers picked us up and were on us almost immediately.

"We had deep water, which extended right up close to Honshu, but sonar conditions can be extraordinarily good some times and this was one of those times. I suppose someone kept track of the number of depth charges that were loosed upon us. But if they did I don't remember the exact number, but my recollection is that about 30 depth charges rained down on us. Many of these were close indeed.

"As usual, we had rigged the ship for silent running and had shut down all possible electrical equipment in order to conserve our batteries. Under these conditions, the ship always took on an eerie aspect. Most of the lights were out — no ventilation was running — people spoke in whispers, if at all, and every sound seemed to reverberate throughout the ship, seemingly loud enough to be heard in Tokyo.

"Things had become so threatening that the captain stationed officers in every compartment ready to supervise on-scene corrective action for whatever mishaps might occur. As assistant gunnery officer, my station was the After Torpedo Room, the last compartment aft and far removed from the command center and the source of the only available information.

71

"We could, of course, hear the screws of the attacking destroyers through the hull as they approached for an attack and then receded to prepare for another. We could roughly judge the proximity of the attack, by the loudness of the screw noises and ensuing explosions, which usually came two at a time.

"The experience was harrowing. Noting that the ship had been running at 500 feet can best convey how close we came to 'death by depth charge'. Just after the worst of the attacks, I read 625 feet on the After Torpedo Room depth gauge. The ship was designed and built to operate down to a maximum depth of 412 feet. Eventually, our attackers lost the scent, and we survived to fight another day, but it was close... a very close call indeed," Axene says with a faraway look, as though reliving the horror of the depth charge attack.

"Life in Parche, under Captain McCrory (Captain Mac), was pretty austere. Life and death submarining against the Japanese was serious business, and the captain took it seriously all the time.

"The wardroom was very quiet. Seldom was there a poker game, a game of acey-deucy, or even a cribbage hand," Axene, said. "We had a very high-quality, multi-band radio, but playing it was frowned upon. Basically, Captain Mac felt that if an officer was not on watch or doing ship's work, he ought to be sleeping to ensure that he would be physically ready for the next combat encounter. I wasn't able to adjust to this regimen very well. I've always enjoyed background music while engaged in other activities, including work, and I feel lost if I can't check the news broadcasts occasionally and find out what is happening in the world around me.

"At the end of what turned out to be our last patrol—Parche's fifth, my second—we set sail for Pearl Harbor on the surface at our normal surface cruising speed of about 14 knots, two engines on the line.

"The weather was good and we were quickly distancing ourselves from Japanese waters, where our patrol had been conducted; and we were busy doing the clean-up chores associated with end-of-patrol. We were scheduled to stop briefly at Pearl Harbor, to fuel and off-load weapons, then proceed on to the states for an overhaul at the Mare Island Naval Shipyard, near San Francisco.

One quiet afternoon, I was alone in the wardroom, working on my section of our patrol report. I donned headphones and tuned to a short wave, English language broadcast. Almost the first thing I heard was that the United States had dropped a super bomb on Japan — a bomb that was reputed to be atomic in nature. According to the report, the bomb had caused a great deal destruction and many deaths.

At that moment, I was the first and only person on board Parche who knew of this significant development," Axene recalled. "Needless to say," he grinned, "I quickly shared my knowledge with others who were up and about, and almost instantly a majority of the crew and officers, including Captain Mac, were monitoring that radio broadcast.

"As additional information was received, including information on the subsequent bomb which was dropped on Nagasaki; it became clear to us all that the war was probably over.

"That, of course, turned out to be the case. Not long after our arrival at Mare Island— about 10 days later— Japan capitulated and World War II came to an end.

"We weren't in San Francisco where the event was really celebrated, but we savored the moment. It was, without question, a real turning point in my life and the lives of the entire Parche crew."

After the war, Rear Admiral Axene went on to serve 33 years in the submarine service, including serving as executive officer of the world's first nuclear-powered submarine the USS Nautilus (SSN-571) when it was placed in commission in 1954. He also served as commanding officer of two nuclear-powered submarines before retiring from the Navy in 1974.

###

Mary Turner:

<u>Unsung Hero</u>

While the men fighting the wars on the battle fields of Europe and the Pacific during World War II pretty well knew what to expect on a day-to-day basis, for those remaining behind, on the home front, It was more often than not a guessing game. Still they struggled along keeping families together and industry running."

In many cases, the wives, mothers and sisters, keeping the home fires burning while the men were fighting in Europe or the Pacific, are the true unsung heroes of World War II.

Would the food and gasoline ration stamps hold out until the end of the month? Could badly needed car and house repairs be put off a little longer? As great as these concerns were, they paled in comparison to the anxiety of not knowing the fate of loved ones. One of those heroes of the home front was Mary Emma Turner of Orange Beach, Alabama.

Turner and her husband, Lieutenant Colonel Doyne Lynell Turner of the Army Air Corps, had only been married a little more than two years when the B-29 Superfortress the colonel was flying in was shot down over Tokyo April 13, 1945.

Although Mary and her husband grew up in the same small town of Dover, Arkansas, and attended the same high school they didn't date until sometime later. "Actually it was my Aunt Nellie who brought us together," Mary remembers. "Lynell, he preferred to be called by his middle name, was my aunt's next-door neighbor her family just loved him. She was certain that sooner or later we would get together.

"After he joined the Army Air Corps he would come home on a pretty regular basis and we would take walks together, go the movies, and things like that. Later after my family moved to Muskogee, Oklahoma, he would fly out to see me. Actually, I think he just liked to show off his flying skills," she said with a laugh.

Whether it was due to his skill as a dashing airman or Aunt Nellie's match making, Mary and Lynell were married in St. Louis, Missouri, in 1943. Their only child, Patricia Ann, was only three months old when Colonel Turner was shot down. Patricia said that although she has no personal memories of her father, she nevertheless feels that she knew him, thanks to her mother.

"From all the stories I've heard about my dad I know he must have been a wonderful, caring person. I wish I could have had the opportunity to have known him when I was growing up." Ironically, Pat may have indeed been able to personally know her dad had Colonel Turner not decided to go along as a passenger on that ill-fated bombing raid over Tokyo.

After completing flight school at Parks Air College in East St. Louis, Illinois, Turner was commissioned in October 1940 and rose rapidly through the ranks, to lieutenant colonel.

By the time America entered the war, the young Dover, Arkansas, aviator had already seen duty in Panama, Washington, D.C., and Walker Army Air Field at Victoria, Kansas, were he trained to command a B-29 squadron.

Following familiarization training in the B-29, Turner and his 458th Bombardment Squadron were assigned to the Guam-based 330th Bombardment Group. It was from here, that the colonel, in his never-ending pursuit to be the perfect commanding officer took off on what would be his last flight.

The 459th's mission that fateful day of April 13, 1945, was to blanket Japan's capital, Tokyo, with incendiary bombs. Although not assigned to fly the mission, Turner went along as an observer.

Two weeks later, Mary received a letter from the 330th Bomb Group chaplain informing her that her husband's plane had been shot down. The whereabouts and status of the crew, including her husband, was unknown. The only other communication Mary had from the Army arrived on June 14, from the commanding general of the Twentieth Air Force confirming what the 330th Bomb Group chaplain had stated earlier. "It was a horrifying experience," Mary recalls. "I didn't know what to expect or who to turn too. I only knew that my sweet wonderful husband, the father of my three-month-old baby girl was missing and somehow, I had to carry on. I was very fortunate that my family was nearby and more than willing to help take care of the baby. Actually," Mary laughs, "they fought over who was going to take care of Pat while I worked."

The news of Lynell being missing in action wasn't the first time that Mary's family had been confronted with bad news from the war zone. A year earlier, Mary's brother-in-law, Ernest, was killed during the Normandy Invasion. "Lynell and I were at a base in Columbus, Ohio," Mary recalls, when we received notice that my sister Iva's husband, Ernest Snapp, had been killed. Iva was visiting her in-laws in Kentucky at the time, so Lynell was asked if he would deliver the message to her. We didn't want to call her with such bad news, so we got in the car and drove all night to deliver the message in person."

While Mary was agonizing over the fate of her husband, and the welfare of her child, the colonel—as she would learn from news accounts after the war—was agonizing over how to stay alive so that he could return to his wife and daughter.

After the war was over, Mary learned that after the B-29 Colonel Turner was flying in was shot down, he was taken prisoner by the Japanese and for a short time held at Kempei Tal headquarters in Tokyo, before being moved to the Tokyo Yoyoge Army Prison, where he was placed in a room of a one-story wooden building with 61 other captured American airmen.

On May 26, the American air forces made an all out aerial assault on Tokyo. Fires caused by the exploding incendiary bombs quickly consumed the wooden buildings of the prison. According to records obtained after the American occupation of Japan, all the American POWs perished in the fire. The records also showed that the lives of the Americans could have possibly been saved had the Japanese guards released them from their burning cells.

Based on testimony given at a military tribunal in Yokohama, Japan, after the war, a few of the POWs did manage to escape the flames only to be cut down by guards with swords as they attempted to flee the wall of flames. Five of the Yoyoge prison guards who refused to release the Americans from their locked cells when the incendiary bombs fell on the prison were charged with the murder of 65 captured American airmen, and sentenced to death by hanging.

Colonel Turner and his fellow American POWs were initially buried in the prison yard, and later removed to the American cemetery at Yokohama, Japan, where most of them, including Turner, still remain.

Mary didn't learn of her husband's death or the horrible circumstances of his death until after the war when she found his name on a casualty list published in a newspaper.

Mary never remarried after the loss of her husband; instead she concentrated on making a life for her and her daughter. "I worked for a business supply firm in Muskogee for several years after the death of my husband," said Mary, and then in 1950 I went into business for myself.

The man I worked for decided he wanted to retire and would like to sell the business so I arranged to buy it."

Mary said the biggest problem she encountered during her early years as a businesswoman, was convincing people that she was the owner. "Salesmen would drop by and the first question they would ask is, 'can I see the man in charge.'"

With the help of her sisters, Mary and many "wonderful employees" operated the Office Appliance Company in Muskogee, until 2000, when, at the instance of her daughter she closed the business after 50 years, and moved to the Alabama Gulf Coast.

Although she was a military wife for only a short time, Mary said she loved every minute of it, especially the time she spent as a Red Cross Gray Lady volunteer at Bolling Army Air Field near Washington, D.C. "I loved helping the boys in the hospital at Bolling Field. I really felt that I was making a contribution."

###

KOREAN WAR

1950-1953

Paul B. Dickson:

Speed Run to Korea

In June 1950, Americans were basking in the glory of peace after the rigors and restrictions of World War II. The economy was booming and thousands of former servicemen were completing college—a reward of sorts for the Allied victory over German and Japan.

Despite the fact that most Americans thought the clouds of war were far behind, one young Floridian, Paul B. Dickson of Bascom, was making a speed run into harm's way.

Dickson was an aerial photographer with VC-62 deployed aboard the aircraft carrier USS Leyte (CV-32).

Leyte was midway through a Mediterranean deployment, when the carrier suddenly received orders to sail for the Pacific. While Dickson and most of the sailors aboard Leyte were trying to make sense of all the stories being generated by the rumor mill, the ship's captain was digesting the official message: In the early morning hours of June 25, 1950, seven assault infantry divisions, a tank brigade and two independent infantry regiments of the North Korean People's Army invaded South Korea. Two days later — June 27 — President Harry S. Truman ordered General of the Army Douglas MacArthur, Commander-in-Chief, Far East Command, to commit American naval and air forces to the support of South Korea.

After a two-day battle —June 28 to 29 —Seoul, the South Korean Capital, was captured by the North Korean Army and the Republic of Korea Army was virtually destroyed. On June 30, following the loss of Seoul, Truman; responding to pleas from the United Nations, authorized the use of U.S. ground forces in Korea and ordered a naval blockade of the Korea coast.

As the magnitude of what was happening began to filter down to Dickson's level, the young sailor was both anxious and nervous. When liberty in the Italian port of Leghorn, Italy was suddenly cancelled and the Leyte put to sea, Dickson and his shipmates knew that rumors of another war were all too real.

"The word got around the ship pretty fast," Dickson, a retired lieutenant commander, recalls. "When the ship got underway from Leghorn with orders to return to the states, we suspected that we would eventually end up in Korea."

"At the time, the Navy had just started assigning two carriers to the Mediterranean. On this particular deployment it was the Leyte and the Coral Sea. We went into port at Beirut, Lebanon, and transferred our Marine detachment to the Coral Sea and got underway for Korea, via Portsmouth, Virginia, and the Panama Canal."

According to a 1950 clipping from Dickson's hometown newspaper, the *Bascom News,* the Leyte entered combat on October 8, 1950 —after a record-breaking 35-day, 8,513-mile speed run from the Mediterranean. Nine of those days, which weren't reported by the newspaper, were spent in drydock at Portsmouth Naval Shipyard.

"Returning to the States from the Mediterranean; we went straight into drydock without unloading ammo or defueling. The squadrons, of course had flown off earlier, but the ship totally bypassed normal procedures and went straight into drydock to have some minor work done before continuing on to the Pacific.

"For the most part," Dickson said "being a shipboard photographer aboard Leyte during the Korean War was rather boring.

"The air crews were of course staying plenty busy. But for the rest of us it was hurry up and wait. We (photographers) maintained VC-63's cameras, loaded film into the magazines, mounted cameras in the airplanes and processed the film when the planes returned. But while we were waiting for the planes to return and, in between flights it got kind of boring," Dickson recalled.

Although Dickson and his fellow photographers may have gotten bored, it was a routine most VC-63 personnel and other squadrons and air crewmen aboard Leyte would have welcomed.

Within hours of entering Korean waters on October 8, 1950, Leyte launched the first of more than 3,000 sorties Leyte aircraft would fly against the North Korea Army and its Chinese allies.

Eleven days after Leyte arrived in Korean waters; it looked like the Korean War would soon be ending.

Having landed at Wonsan, the Americans began a drive toward the Yalu River, the boundary between Korea and Manchuria. By the end of October the South Korean Army — with United Nations support — had killed or captured more than 135,000 North Korean troops, virtually dissolving the enemy force.

By early November a UN victory seemed assured. Most encounters with what was left of the North Korean Army ended in victory for the UN forces. Then suddenly and without warning, China entered the war on the side of North Korea.

While Dickson wasn't actually involved in ground or aerial combat, he did, nevertheless, have some tense moments... like the time when he was placed on report for dereliction of duty.

"One day me and another photographer were installing a K-18 camera on an airplane when the other guy dropped a small, green notebook into the camera. In the meantime I went back to the lab to load the film magazine.

"When I got back topside," he continued, "the leading petty officer said everything had been checked out and the launch was ready to go. Well," Dickson continued, "when the flight returned I retrieved the film magazine and took it below to process the film. When I was finished and turned the lights on, there was nothing on the film except for a few irregular spots."

While the photo chief, photo officer and intelligence officer scratched their heads trying to solve the problem of the botched film, Dickson, who had only recently been advanced to third class petty officer concluded that something had been dropped into the camera body prior to the magazine being mounted.

"I think I know what the problem is," I told the chief. The four of us, along with the leading petty officer and the photographer who helped me mount the camera in the plane all went up to the flight deck. There, just as I thought, were the remnants of a notebook. Gee, I thought, this is great. I'll surely get a Letter of Appreciation for solving this problem. Instead of a Letter of Appreciation," Dickson laughed, "I was given 30 hours of extra duty.

"I couldn't believe it! Why, I asked the chief, am I being punished? It's not my notebook. I solved the problem. 'Well', the chief said, 'you were the petty officer who put the magazine on. You should have checked it.'

"But the leading petty officer was right there, I protested. This isn't right. I'll take captain's mast before I'll accept extra duty." I was all set to go mast, but my buddy called me aside and told me it was his notebook and pleaded with me to accept the extra duty. He was afraid that if the photo officer found out that the notebook was his, he wouldn't be recommended for third class... I took the 30 hours."

Following the Korean War, Dickson continued his Navy career and saw duty during the Vietnam War as commanding officer of Pacific Fleet Combat Camera Group.

He retired from the Navy and naval photography in 1978, after 30 years of service.

###

Art Grebe:
<u>Flying Leatherneck</u>

When young Art Grebe was studying world geography in his central Montana one-room school house, he probably got his first exposure to a small Asian country known as Korea.

He probably learned little more about Korea than its form of government and what its major export was. Little did he realize that one day he would be flying over its fields and mountains in a Corsair aircraft as an enlisted fighter pilot with the United States Marine Corps — an action that would earn him the Distinguished Flying Cross.

"We were bombing some warehouses," Grebe recalls, "when our leader (the squadron executive officer) started spilling fluid out of his Corsair. He shut his oil coolers off but that didn't work. He'd been hit. A minute or so later his engine froze up and he crashed into a rice paddy. I stayed low and I saw a group of North Koreans heading toward his aircraft.

"I fired a few rounds into the mud right in front of them," Grebe says, "and they stopped suddenly and started acting like they were working in the rice paddies. With his radio still intact the executive officer told me to quit flying over the village because they were shooting at me.

"I just kept circling and kept everybody away from him until some P-51s had us in sight. Once they took over and the pilot was picked up by chopper, they destroyed the aircraft. I remember one of the P-51 pilots jokingly saying, 'I always wanted to shoot up a Corsair.'"

Grebe took off for the nearest airfield. "I went straight in because I was low on fuel. I touched down, taxied in to the ramp—and the engine died. I had cut it a little close."

Grebe grew up with two brothers and a sister on a small farm on Rattlesnake Creek near the town of Sumatra, Montana. It was here while walking to school and working on his dad's farm that

Grebe spent hours watching eagles and hawks soaring—and dreaming of flying like Charles Lindbergh.

In 1936 a severe drought which included the central Montana area forced the Grebe family to relocate to Belfry, Montana, near Yellowstone National Park.

After settling in to his new surroundings, Grebe sent off for a correspondence course to learn how to fly airplanes, but eventually gave up on that notion. With his aviation career temporarily abandoned, the strapping 15-year-old settled into a typical farm-life routine; up no later than 6 a.m. to feed the pigs and chickens and milk the cows by kerosene lantern.

Following chores; Grebe settled down to a hearty home-cooked breakfast and then walked to school.

That was Grebe's routine until his graduation from high school in 1939, when he began working on ranches for a year and a half.

Grebe says he would have liked to have gone to college after high school graduation, but working on the family farm was a priority. Then the war came along.

With many of his friends enlisting, Grebe followed suit — signing on with the Marine Corps in June 10, 1942. "I had wanted to join the Marine Corps even before Pearl Harbor," remembers Grebe, "but my dad talked me out of it. I had liked the idea of getting into a sea and land service— I didn't want to be just aboard ship."

Grebe eventually went to clerical school and wound up being sent to St. Thomas in the Virgin Islands with VMS-3. "We were tasked with looking for German subs in the Caribbean. We were also keeping an eye on the French fleet near Martinique. The government believed the base was being used to refuel German submarines, but we could never prove it," says Grebe.

In 1944 his squadron was decommissioned and he returned to the states, where he promptly put in for flight training—and was accepted. In 1947, then Staff Sgt. Grebe was designated a Naval Aviation Pilot and assigned to VMF-312 in Korea.

"We did road reconnaissance and close air support," Grebe said. "You'd show up over a target and they'd start sending up bursts of flak... and lots of small arms fire. I liked flying close air support the best because you could definitely see what you had accomplished.

"I preferred the early morning flights. That way if a pilot got shot down he had more daylight to get rescued or find his way back to friendly territory. A good breakfast was important too. I always ate breakfast with the mess cooks," smiled Grebe.

"One day a mess sergeant came in and told me to do something. I looked at him funny and he realized I wasn't one of is mess cooks. He asked me what I was doing in there and I told him I had an early flight and had come in to eat. The rest of the mess cooks cracked up over that because here was a staff sergeant asking a master sergeant to do something. I don't know why he didn't see my rate insignia on my utilities— I think he may have been a little drunk."

At the end of the Korea war Grebe returned to Cherry Point, North Caroline, and was reassigned to fly jets. I wanted speed," he smiled, "and those props jobs flew way too slow." After several more changes of duty stations, Grebe retired from the Marine Corps in 1965.

###

Charley Wise:

Joined the Navy to Avoid Foxholes

When Charley Wise joined the Navy in 1947 as a hospital corps-man it would be easy to believe that is was for a variety of noble rea-sons —to serve his fellow man, attend to the sick and suffering, etc. Actually, according to the retired senior chief hospital corpsman, it was a small matter of deceit that put him in the naval hospital corps and a tour of duty in Korea with the First Marine Division.

"My dad had been drafted during War World II and was sta-tioned at Jacksonville," said the Cottondale, Florida native. "So I had some familiarity with the Navy. So one day, me and two of my buddies, decided we wanted to join the Navy too. Of course we quickly discovered it wasn't going to be as easy as we had thought. We were all three underage. They were both 17 and I was 16.

For his 17-year-old buddies getting into the Navy was a simple matter of getting at least one of their parents to sign for them. But for 16-year-old Charles Hughprice Wise it was a little more complicat-ed.

"I had always been called Charles Hughprice Wise when I was a kid," Wise said. "But on my birth certificate my name was listed as Charley. So rather than show my birth certificate to the recruiter, I got the principal of my high school to sign an affidavit which said my name was Charles Wise and my year of birth was 1930."

Now that Wise had the necessary "proof" of age his next problem was getting his parents to go along with his grand plan.

"My dad was stationed at Jacksonville and didn't have any real problems with it," Wise recalls, "but mom wasn't so sure. 'Look at it this way, mom,' I told her, 'I'm going to be drafted in a couple of years anyway. This way I get to pick the service I want to go into and if there is another war, I will be a lot safer aboard a ship than I would be in a foxhole.' That was all the convincing she needed. So with affidavit —signed by the principal, a few friends and several neighbors— off I went to the Navy Recruiting Office.

"Cottondale is a small community and the recruiter suspected that I wasn't 17. But I didn't show him a birth certificate and according to the affidavit I provided, I was 17 and I had my mom's signature. Still, the recruiter warned me that if I wasn't telling the truth I could go to jail for five years. At that point I almost chickened out. But after a couple of seconds I decided, 'what the heck' I've come this far, I may as well go all the way."

A short time later, while going through recruit training in San Diego, Wise, like the rest of his fellow recruits, was sent to the classification office to see what they were qualified for.

"I wanted to be an electrician," Wise said, "but my math scores weren't high enough. 'You can be a hospital corpsman or you can go to sea as a boatswain's mate,' the classifier told me. Hospital corpsman looked pretty darn good," Wise laughed.

One day while going through Hospitalman "A" School, Wise said he saw what he thought was a Marine wearing a Navy rating badge.

"I hadn't been in the Navy very long, but I had been in long enough to know that sailors didn't wear Marine uniforms. 'Why is that Marine wearing a Navy rating badge?' I asked a chief. 'He's not a Marine, the chief said,' 'he's one of us.' That was the first time that I realized that Navy hospital corpsmen served with the Marines, and when doing so, they were required to wear Marine Corps uniforms."

Suddenly the statement he had made to his mother about spending his service time in relative comfort aboard a ship didn't seem so sound anymore. For the first time in his short Navy career, Wise realized that as a hospital corpsman there was a very real possibility that he too, could spend some time in a foxhole.

On January 31, 1950, he came a step closer to "humping the boonies" when he reported to the Headquarters Battalion of the First Marine Division in Korea.

"That was about the safest place in the division. This is where the commanding general, the band and medical personnel were assigned," Wise said.

"Occasionally I would see a first aid man (corpsman assigned to a combat unit) come into sickbay wearing grenades and a three or four day growth of beard, swaggering and looking real macho. That's what I wanted to be... a first aid man," Wise, his eyes brightening, recalls.

His wish came true a short time later.

"I guess it must have been a couple of weeks after that, that the battalion received a request from an infantry company for a replacement for its corpsman. Three of us volunteered and for some reason I was selected."

At first Wise was assigned to a reconnaissance squad but after a few months he was transferred to a combat unit.

"In those days, recon didn't do any combat stuff, except in self-defense. We would go out on patrol and when we found the enemy we would radio their position back to an infantry group and continue our patrol."

On one early morning patrol, Wise and his recon patrol waded across a shallow river. In a matter of minutes they were pinned down in deep snow.

"Laying there in the snow, cold, wet and scared, I was beginning to have second thoughts about the macho stuff," Wise said. "I figured I had made a mistake by leaving the warmth and comfort of the battalion. But by then it was too late to do anything about it. Once you were in a field unit there was no going back."

A short time later, due to heavy losses by the 3rd Marine Regiment, Wise was transferred to an infantry division where he served out the remainder of his 11-month tour in Korea.

Despite the fact that Wise was involved in several skirmishes he managed to return home with only a minor knee injury and went on to serve more than 20 years in the Navy, including a tour of duty as an independent duty hospital corpsman aboard a minesweeper. He retired from active duty as a Senior Chief Hospital Corpsman in August 1968.

"I enjoyed my tour with the Marines," Wise said, "but I have some doubts about our involvement in Korea. I guess that's why people try to forget it. But you can bet those of us who were there will never forget it."

###

Stan E. Toy:
<u>**The Fourth of July**</u>

Ask most Americans where and how they observed the Fourth of July in 1950 and they will probably scratch their head and respond with a blank stare. Ask that same question of retired Navy Senior Chief Photographer's Mate Stan E. Toy and he'll tell you exactly how he and his shipmates observed Independence Day aboard the USS Valley Forge (CV-45) in 1950.

On June 25, 1950, the North Korean Army poured across the 38th parallel and quickly captured the South Korean capital of Seoul.

The Valley Forge, one of two carriers operating in the South China Sea at the time had just dropped anchor in Hong Kong Harbor. Toy and his fellow photo mates were preparing to go on liberty when the word was passed over the ship's address system that liberty was cancelled and the ship was getting underway immediately. "We didn't know what was going on," Toy, a World War II veteran, said, "but we knew it had to be something big for us get underway so soon after dropping anchor."

From Hong Kong the Valley Forge steamed at top speed for Subic Bay, Philippines. After replenishing in Subic Bay, Valley Forge made a speed run north to the Yellow Sea area.

"Within minutes of leaving Subic Bay we went to general quarters" Toy recalls. "We (the ship) were shorthanded so nearly all the photo mates were assigned to gun crews.

"The normal battle station for photographers of course is the photo lab. But this wasn't a normal situation. Me and three other photographers — Ted Gibson, Francis Bell and Bob Ariaga — were assigned to a 40mm gun crew on the fantail, probably the worst possible place to be on an aircraft carrier, and that's pretty much where we stayed for the next several days," Toy said.

"We slept at our GQ station and took turns going to the mess decks to eat. We still didn't understand the seriousness of what was really happening until the morning a chief gunner's mate gave us a briefing. 'Many of you fellows have never been in combat,' he began. 'So listen up. If you see one of your shipmates get hit, don't pay any attention to him. You keep your mind on your job. We've got people trained to look after your buddies.'

"That's when it finally hit me that this was for real. We were once again involved in a war."

The date was July 4, 1950.

The Fourth of July is normally observed as holiday routine (a more relaxed time than normal) when ships are at sea but life aboard the Valley Forge on July 4, 1950 was anything but routine.

"Although we were at general quarters, the cooks had prepared a holiday meal. Turkey and dressing, ham... A real Thanksgiving meal," Toy recalled. "Only thing was, we had to eat in shifts because we were at general quarters."

According to the retired Navy photographer, only one man at a time from his gun crew was allowed to leave his station for chow and even then the amount of time they could spend on the mess deck was limited.

"I had just got my food and set down," Toy said, "when the general alarm sounded. 'General quarters, general quarters, this is not a drill; this is not a drill. Bogies approaching from the starboard side.' "I didn't even know what a bogie was," Toy laughed. I thought they were talking about Humphery Bogart. Anyway, as I said, I was just about ready to dig into my turkey and dressing, when the GQ alarm was sounded. I grabbed a handful of stuffing, shoved it in my mouth, stuck a turkey leg in my shirt and took off for my battle station on the fantail."

Reaching his gun station, Toy scanned the starboard horizon to get a look at the incoming bogies.

"I saw what looked like about 40 little black specks coming our way," Toy said. "At about the same time the ship launched the CAP (combat air patrol). The tin cans (destroyers) started firing. About that time, one of the guys in the gun crew said, 'Oh my God!'

"I turned and looked in the direction that he was pointing and there was our helicopter in the water smoking. 'Christ', I screamed, they came in so fast I didn't even see them. Actually the helo had suffered some engine trouble and went down. But at the time, we thought he had been shot down," Toy recalls.

"At about that same time one of the destroyers started dropping depth charges. Rumors quickly spread throughout the ship that we were being tracked by a submarine."

Senior Chief Toy said that he learned years later that there had been no confirmed reports of submarines in the area. Actually the destroyer's depth charge attack was attributed to a combination of jitters and a false alarm. As far as the bogies were concerned, when the tin cans opened fire, they turned and left the area.

Later in the afternoon on July 4, 1950, aircraft launched earlier in the day from Valley Forge were returning. One of the planes, an AD Corsair, had its tailhook shot away during an air strike. Rather than ditch in the water, the decision was made to rig the barrier and bring him aboard. The idea was to use the plane for spare parts.

"We (the gun crew) watched the plane make its approach. It crossed over the round down; we heard the 'thump' of his wheels as they hit the deck, then for several seconds, nothing. Then all of a sudden we hear this god-awful crash. The plane hit the deck pretty hard and actually bounced over the barrier and smacked into several parked aircraft. The pilot got out OK and we had our spare parts. They were scattered all over the flight deck," Toy laughed.

As far as holiday routine was concerned. It was a day that the retired senior chief has recalled each Fourth of July since. But Toy also recalls that he was one the fortunate ones in his gun crew. He had a turkey leg in his shirt that he nibbled on most of July 4, 1950.

###

CUBAN MISSILE CRISIS
October–September

1962

Art Giberson:

The **Brink** of Nuclear War

Between the 1953 uneasy truce in Korea and full-scale military involvement in Vietnam in 1965, America's armed forces were called upon to protect America and its interests around the world numerous times— any one of which could have escalated into a global conflict.

But none came as close to pushing the world to the brink of a nuclear holocaust as the Cuban Missile Crisis in the closing months of 1962.

Petty Officer Second Class Art Giberson and his shipmates aboard the Mayport, Florida-based destroyer USS Zellars (DD-777) were there for the duration.

Zellars, affectionately referred to as the Zippin' Z, had departed Mayport on March 9, 1962 for what was supposed to have been a seven-month deployment of the Mediterranean. After months at sea and port calls to such exotic places as Hydra Bay and Athens, Greece; Menton, France; Barcelona, Spain; Chahbar, Iran; Karachi, Pakistan; Djibouti, French Somaliland; and Naples, Italy Zellars returned to Mayport on October 2, for what Giberson and the rest of the crew thought would be a well-deserved inport period with their families.

"After an uneventful seven-month deployment and unbelievably nice weather and calm seas for that time of the year in the Atlantic, we actually arrived back in American waters nearly a week ahead of schedule," Giberson recalled. "The thinking was, of course, that we were going to get home a few days early. But because the Navy is a stickler for schedules, that wasn't to be. When the ship was just a couple of hundred miles from Mayport, the skipper, Commander James E. Murphy, came on the 1mc (ship's address system) and announced that he had been ordered to slow the ship down so that we would arrive as scheduled on October 2.

"After several days of streaming in circles, conducting mindless war games, and cleaning the ship from stem to stern for the umpteenth time, we finally steamed into Mayport, right on schedule, where families and friends waited on the pier."

While his shipmates scanned the crowd of several hundred people milling about on the pier for a glimpse of a loved one, Giberson was below decks packing for a bus trip to Baltimore, Maryland, where his wife, Jean and two sons, Eugene and Johnny, were waiting.

Within an hour of docking, Giberson, along with most of the ship's crew had departed the ship on leave or liberty. Zellars was scheduled to remain in port for the remainder of 1962. The Zellars next extended period away from its homeport would be a six-month shipyard overhaul at Charleston, South Carolina. But after nearly seven months at sea even the thought of the looming yard period failed to dampen the high morale of the destroyermen. Charleston, After all, was an easy drive for those sailors wishing to return to Mayport on weekends.

"After a week or so in Baltimore, where my wife and boys had remained while the Zippin' Z was in the Med, I loaded the family in my old '58 Plymouth and we drove to Mayport where I had rented a mobile home. We got to Mayport around the 11th or 12th of October, if I recall correctly," the former destroyerman said. "But I do remember that we had only been in Mayport a couple of days before all hell broke loose.

"I can't recall the exact date, but I believe it was probably around October 13 or 14, but I do know that it was on a Saturday morning. Jean, the boys and I were leaving the trailer park to go grocery shopping. But before we could get out of the park a Duval County Sheriff's deputy stopped us.

"You assigned to one of the ships at Mayport," the deputy asked, pointing to the station decal on the front bumper of my car.

"Yeah," I answered, "what's up?"

"I don't know," the deputy said, "but the Navy requested that we assist the Shore Patrol in rounding you guys up. You're supposed to report back to your ships."

As I drove Jean and the boys back to the trailer, I met another guy, from the ship, Stan Ross, who lived next door to me, on his way out of the mobile home park. He flagged me down and asked if I had gotten the word about reporting back to the ship. "Yeah," I told him. "My wife doesn't drive so I'm going to take her and the boys back home and I'll be right behind you."

Returning to the ship, Giberson, Ross and dozens of other sailors tried in vain to find out what was going on. After about three hours or so, Capt. Murphy came on the 1mc and announced that the ship had just completed a readiness drill called by Commander, Naval Forces Jacksonville. With that brief announcement the crew was allowed to go back on liberty.

"Unannounced drills wasn't uncommon in those days," Giberson says, "so everyone went on about their business. When I got home, Jean washed the kids and we went on with our grocery shopping.

"The next morning, a Sunday, I was awakened by a loud pounding on the door. I remember looking at the clock and was surprised to see that it was only 6 a.m. I got up, went to the door and was confronted by still another deputy and a Shore Patrolman."

"All military personnel are being ordered back to their stations," the Shore Patrolman said

"Thinking that it was just another drill that probably would be over within a hour or so, I asked Ross if he and his wife would like to ride to the base with Jean, the boys and I, and afterward we could all go to brunch together. After all, Jean didn't drive and there was really no reason to take two cars.

"We drove to the base and were lucky enough to find a parking spot right at the head of the pier. Kissing our wives and saying bye to the boys, Ross and I headed for the ship. We should be back in about an hour, I remember saying as we got out of the car."

Reporting aboard the officer of the day told us to prepare to get underway. "Get underway! Where are we going?" I asked the OOD.

"Don't know." He answered. "All liberty has been cancelled and we're getting underway as soon as the captain arrives."

War Stories

'Aha, it's just another drill," Ross announced loudly, showing his frustration. "Let's get a cup of coffee. Liberty call will probably be announced before we finish the cup,' Ross said.

Twenty minutes or so later, all lines were cast off and the ship slowly moved away from the pier as the Giberson and Ross families watched in disbelieve... thank goodness Stan's wife could drive.

After clearing the channel, Captain Murphy's voice came over the 1mc. "Now hear this! This is the captain speaking. All ships in the Jacksonville area have been put on alert and ordered to put to sea. Regrettably, I don't have a lot of information to share with you at this time. I expect to hear from ComNavFor (Commander Naval Forces) Jacksonville later today. I will keep you informed as information becomes available."

"The captain's voice had hardly faded away before our leading chief charged through the door of the shipfitters shop. 'Peterson, Giberson,' he said in a loud voice. 'The captain wants a couple of machine gun brackets mounted on each side of the bridge. The gunner's mates will meet you on the bridge and show you where to place them.'

"Machine gun mounts! For what?" Shipfitter Second Class Gerry (Pete) Peterson, the senior shipfitter asked.

"The chief just shook his head and said, 'I don't know any more than you do. Just get your welding gear and get up to the bridge.'

"When we reached the bridge we were met by a gunner's mate, I believe his name was Whittle. Anyway, he provided Pete and I with a couple of metal brackets and showed us where they were to be mounted. Just as we were finishing up the XO (executive officer) Lieutenant Commander William Gatts arrived on the bridge. Excuse me Mr. Gatts, I asked. What's going on sir? Are we going to war or something?"

Gatts kinda looked out over the open sea as green water broke over the bow and said, without any emotion whatsoever, "I don't know. But there's a good possibility that we might do just that. Right now I'm more concerned about this weather and the fact that

97

half the crew is on leave," he said as another huge wave broke over the bow. Weather guessers say we may be heading directly into the path of a tropical storm."

"After a few of days at sea the Zippin' Z returned to Mayport to take on fuel. Normally we would have refueled from a tanker at sea, but the heavy weather the XO had had been worried about earlier was now a full-fledged hurricane named Ella with winds of 115 mph which would have put both ships in great danger. Being only a hundred miles or so offshore, the skipper decided it would be best to return to Mayport to refuel. The ship would only to be in port for a few hours and no one would be allowed to leave the ship except on official business.

"R Division had nothing do with the refueling process, so I figured if I could get off the ship, maybe I could sneak home for an hour or so. I knew the shop was getting low on welding gear and there was a supply depot at Mayport, so why not give it a try. I filled out a supply form for a box of welding rods, forged the chief's signature and as soon as the ship tied up I headed for the quarterdeck. I thought I had it made until I saw who the OOD was—Chief Beauchamp, the R Division leading chief. Knowing the phony welding rod request wasn't going to work, I simply asked the chief if I could leave the ship to call my wife.

'You've got 10 minutes. There's a bank of phones at the head of the pier.'

"I couldn't believe my eyes as I walked toward the phone bank. Heavy military hardware was all over the place. By this time I had been in the Navy for about seven years and I had never seen so much military equipment: tanks, armored personnel carriers, jeeps and trucks in one place. They were everywhere. That's when I realized that something big was about to happen. This wasn't a drill. Then it occurred to me that Jean and the boys could possibly be in grave danger.

"When I got my wife on the phone she told me she had heard something on the radio about Soviet missiles in Cuba. When I got back to the ship I relayed this information to Chief Beauchamp. He nodded and said the president was supposed to address the nation later that night. It was October 22, 1962."

Refueled and replenished Zellars once again departed Mayport without the crew having any knowledge of why we were leaving again, or how long we would be gone.

"We had been back at sea about four hours, I guess, when Captain Murphy announced that the president (John F. Kennedy) would be making an important announcement later that evening and all hands were encouraged to listen, including those on watch, if there was a radio in their watch area. I remember the captain ending his talk by saying the president's address may well be the most important speech we would ever listen to.

"After we finished eating chow that evening, or perhaps I should say, try to eat, while fighting to keep our food trays from sliding off the table as the ship pitched and rolled, every man on the ship staked out a spot to hear the president's speech. As we waited, talk amongst the crew ranged from a pending nuclear attack by Russia to an invasion of Cuba. Come to thank of it, I don't guess any of us knew how close we had come to actually guessing the truth.

Around 7 p.m. the unmistakable voice of President Kennedy could be heard coming from every radio addresses system on the ship. I don't think a single person moved during the next 20 minutes or so as we listened to President Kennedy tell the nation that the United States had 'unmistakable evidence' that Soviet missile sites were being erected in Cuba. As a result, the armed forces had been placed on the highest alert and the Navy was to intercept and inspect all ships bound for Cuba. Ships carrying any materials, which could be used for military purposes, were to be denied entry to Cuban ports. The Navy, the president continued, was to use whatever force necessary to enforce the blockade.

"The president had no more than finished his speech when the general alarm was sounded. Captain Murphy came on the 1mc and told us that we could expect to remain at a modified general quarters (battle stations) until further notice. Now I knew what the machine gun mounts were for.

"A day or so later Zellars and another Mayport-based destroyer joined up with the carrier USS Lexington to provide plane guard and anti-submarine services. Our biggest concern wasn't the fact that we could be going in harm's way, but the lack of information we were getting. I'm sure the skipper and the XO knew what was going on, but for the most part, the crew was clueless. For all we knew, Florida could have been reduced to cinders. The folks back home, of course, knew exactly what was going on. The media was reporting everything that was happening, including our whereabouts. But we were completely in the dark.

I'm sure Captain Murphy had his reasons, but all news of what was actually happening was blacked out aboard the Zippin' Z.

"For the most part things were pretty normal for the first day or so of the blockade. Hurricane Ella had moved up the East Coast making landfall somewhere along the coast of South Carolina making life a lot easier for the crew of the Zippin'Z and the more than 200 other U.S. Navy warships on station in the Atlantic, Caribbean and Gulf of Mexico. During those first few days we didn't encounter any foreign ships and as the weather improved, the carrier returned to normal flight operations.

"Then... I believe it was the night of October 24... sonar picked up a contact. It didn't take more than a couple of minutes to confirm that the contact was a submarine and it wasn't one of ours. We stayed on the sub's tail for most of the night. Actually, it didn't seem to make any effort to try and evade us. It was almost as though it knew we wouldn't attack. The sub's position of course was reported and we were told to maintain contact but not to do anything expect in self-defense. Sometime shortly after dawn the sonar pinging suddenly stopped— the sub was gone.

"Later that day, we made sonar contact a second time. I don't know if it was the same sub or not, but it was a Soviet submarine. Again the task force commander was notified and again Zellars was told to maintain contact but to take no offensive action. Later a radioman told me that the actual message said not to take any action until the USS Joseph P. Kennedy arrived on scene. The Kennedy was named in honor of the president's brother, a Navy pilot killed during World War II. According to the rumors, if indeed they were rumors, the president wanted the Kennedy to have the honor of being the first ship to engage the submarine. It was several hours before the Kennedy arrived on station and by that time the sub was long gone.

"This cat and mouse game continued for about six weeks until the Russians finally decided that missile sites in Cuba wasn't worth a nuclear war and removed them.

I don't recall exactly how long we were deployed for the Cuban Missile Crisis, but after having just returned from a seven-month Mediterranean deployment, it seemed like an eternity. Somewhere around the middle part of November, we were cut loose and returned home.

Before being released from the carrier we went alongside to take on fuel. As a token of his appreciation the Lexington skipper, Capt. Lucien Powell, had 25 gallons of ice cream highland over to us— payment in full for anti-submarine and plane guard services.

"Two other events, other than the fact that the world had literally been on the verge of total destruction, which stand out in my recollection of the Cuban Missile Crisis, is being promoted to first class petty officer and being selected for photo school.

###

VIETNAM

1965–1975

Leonard B. Keller:

Heroes of Ap Bac

In May 1967, Leonard B. Keller was a 19-year-old draftee serving with the "Wild Ones" of Company A, 3rd Battalion, 60th Infantry, 9th Infantry Division in South Vietnam, when he and another young soldier, Private First Class Raymond R. Wright from Moriah, New York, were thrust into the unlikely role of heroes.

On May 2, 1967, the Wild Ones were making a sweep through the Dien Thoung Province in the Mekong Delta of South Vietnam. According to intelligence Company A had received, the Ap Bac area, which the Wild Ones had just moved into; contained a sizeable enemy force —a force the brigade commander hoped to catch and destroy.

After months of chasing the enemy, there was a feeling of elation among the troops. At last the 9th Division was about to meet the enemy on its own terms. But as was with many "well devised" plans in Vietnam things didn't go quite as planned.

To prevent the enemy from withdrawing as the Americans advanced the Brigade Commander, Colonel William Fulton, was hoping to utilize two helicopter companies he had been promised for the Ap Bac operation to make an airmobile assault and to cut off the most likely enemy escape routes. Formed up and waiting at the helicopter pickup site, it soon became apparent that the promised helicopters weren't going to arrive on schedule ...if at all. After several hours of waiting, Fulton decided that if there was to be any chance for a successful operation the brigade would have to move. Company A would be trucked to the AP Bac area and act as the battalion reserve near the line of departure. In the meantime, two other companies already on the line would start the operation by attacking several objectives to the north. The 3rd Battalion, 47th infantry, would join the advance when it arrived in the area.

The terrain in the Ap Bac area, as Keller recalls, consisted mostly of rice paddies surrounded by narrow earthen dikes that could only be crossed at certain points. After several hours of searching their sector for the reported enemy force, the Wild Ones had come up empty.

Only a few people had been seen in the daylong sweep, despite the fact that there were a number of houses visible.

"It was beginning to look like the whole operation was going to be a cake walk," Keller said. That "cake walk" was about to come to an abrupt end.

While Keller and his buddies of the 9th Infantry were counting their blessings, their counterparts in the 47th Infantry, a short distance away, had come under heavy automatic weapons and mortar fire.

Receiving intense fire from all sides and suffering from a large number of casualties, the 47th had temporarily ceased to be an effective fighting force.

Learning that the 47th had made contact with the enemy, the commanding officer of the 3/60th directed B Company— followed by A Company— to move in to assist the 47th. While B Company maneuvered into position to block the enemy's escape, A Company continued to advance. By late afternoon the company had reached the designated restraining line and was deployed in an assault formation, three platoons abreast. Although the company had periodically received light small-arms fire, they had suffered no serious casualties. Within an hour everything was ready for a coordinated attack.

"The plan was to move to within 500 meters of the North Vietnamese/Viet Cong position and overwhelm the enemy with firepower and make an all out assault before the enemy could recover," Keller recalled. "By the time all units were in position for the attack, commanders faced another problem, but one we could use to our advantage —darkness."

"With the light fading fast, it became clear that the daylong battle was about to reach its climax. The air was filled with smoke and small-arms fire, making it impossible for us to advance across the open, dry rice paddies. Realizing that the only way to move forward would be with a split force, a platoon leader divided the unit and directed it to approach the enemy from different directions.

As one squad worked its way down the dike, the squad leader was killed by fire from a bunker along the dike, bringing the squad to a sudden stop. Seeing the squad leader go down, Keller turned to his buddy, Private First Class Raymond R. Wright. "Come on Ray," Keller recalls saying to his friend, "We've come too far to quit now, let's go get them.'"

Leaping to the top of the dike, in plain view of the enemy, Keller and Wright, armed with light machine guns, charged the enemy bunkers. They quickly destroyed an automatic rifle position and a machine gun post and proceeded to penetrate the enemy's main position, taking out an enemy mortar. While Keller emptied his weapon into the bunker, Wright finished off the enemy with a grenade. With the first bunker out of action, Keller and Wright went for a second enemy position and quickly put it out of action. They then turned their attention to a third bunker, containing the machine gun, which had been instrumental in pinning down the squad and killing the squad leader.

Neutralizing that machine gun, Keller and Wright continued their two-man assault on four other bunkers as they ran the length of the dike, which had foxholes every few meters, destroying one enemy position after another. The ferocity of their assault carried Keller and Wright well beyond the enemy line, forcing the enemy to flee. Not satisfied with forcing the enemy from the area, Keller and Wright, spewing a hell of gunfire, gave chase.

When their ammo was totally exhausted, Keller and Wright returned to their platoon and assisted in the evacuation of the wounded. The rest of the platoon was so inspired by the performance of the two teenage soldiers, that they took up the attack and destroyed most of the remaining enemy troops in close, mostly hand-to-hand combat.

"When Ray and I got behind their lines, they became completely disorganized," said Keller. "They (Viet Cong) thought reinforcements had been brought in and were attacking from behind," Keller smiles. "Overall, we lost of good number of our guys at Ap Bac but our casualties were light compared to the losses for the Viet Cong, who lost more than 200 men during the 13-hour engagement."

Keller and Wright survived the Battle of Ap Bac without so much as a scratch and both were awarded the Medal of Honor for their "heroism and indomitable fighting spirit."

Sergeant Keller and Specialist 4th Class Wright were awarded the Medal of Honor by President Lyndon B. Johnson in a White House ceremony on September 19, 1968. It marked the first time that two individuals, from the same unit, had been awarded the Medal of Honor for the same action.

Looking back on that long day at Ap Bac, Keller, a native of Rockford, Illinois, says he doesn't consider himself a hero. "What Ray and I did that day probably wasn't very smart, and I certainly don't recommend it. But at the time we didn't think much about it. We had been taking fire for most of the day, a lot of friends had been killed or wounded, we were scared, tired and hungry. To tell you the truth, we were pissed. Taking out those bunkers was something that needed to be done, and by the grace of God, Ray and I managed to get the job done without getting hurt."

###

James L. Townsend:

The Green Gnats of the Mekong Delta

A gnat, as every Southerner knows, is a pesky little insect with a vicious bite. That definition amply describes the role of the olive-green swift boats that patrolled the rivers and bayous of the Mekong Delta region of South Vietnam during the Vietnam War. Often referred to as the "Brown Water Navy" this fleet of mostly 31-foot, water-jet-propelled, fiberglass hull boats denied the Viet Cong and North Vietnamese access to the hundreds of miles of waterways of South Vietnam. The swift boats, pound for pound, were among the most heavily armed U.S. Navy vessels to take part in the Vietnam War.

The mission of the "brown water Navy" was simple. Interdict the flow of men and materials from the north into the south. The Navy's fleet of PBRs (river patrol boats) with their shallow draft and high speed were ideally suited for the hit-and-run tactics required to stem the flow of water traffic into the south and inflect as much damage as possible on the enemy. One of the men responsible for inflicting that damage was Valdosta, Georgia, native James L. Townsend.

Townsend was a radioman stationed at the Naval Communications Station, Washington, D.C., in 1965 when a Navy wide message came out asking for volunteers to serve in Vietnam.

"We were a small department," Townsend recalls, "most of the enlisted guys were E-5 and above, so it quickly became a macho thing —I'll volunteer if you'll volunteer. So we all volunteered; never really believing that we would actually be sent to Vietnam."

A few weeks later, Townsend was at home listening to a high school football game on the radio when the phone rings. The caller, the Naval Communications Station, command duty officer, told Townsend that he was calling to let him know that his orders for Vietnam had come through. "I thought it was a joke," Townsend, said. "I mean, here I was, just one of hundreds of radiomen in the Navy. It had to be joke." But the joke, as it turned out, was on Townsend. He was on his way to Southeast Asia.

After making arrangements to relocate his wife Betty, and their two children to his hometown of Valdosta, Townsend, then a chief petty officer, departed for Coronado, California, for weapons and survival training. A few weeks later he found himself along with 48 other sailors at Saigon's Tan Son Nhut Air Base.

"Arrival in Vietnam was sort of a rude awakening," Townsend said. Everyone wanted us, but nobody knew what to do with us. Our boats weren't even in country yet. My original orders had me reporting to River Squadron Five.

Actually, about the time that I arrived in Vietnam, the squadron was just being formed up in San Diego."

While waiting for their boats to arrive, Townsend and the others were assigned to a couple of steel-hull boats operating out of Saigon for river operational training. From Saigon he was sent to a newly established base at Bung Tau to await the arrival of the PBRs.

"At the time I still thought that as a radioman, I would eventually be assigned to a communications billet in Saigon. But once we got the boats operational I was asked if I would take over as a patrol officer. I guess that was one of the few times that I was ever 'asked' if I would do something, Townsend laughed. "It took me a while to realize that I was now fully responsible for the lives of eight other men.

On Easter Sunday, 1966, Townsend and his boats, PBR-17 and PBR-21, made their first patrol.

"We would generally run two day patrols from 6 a.m. to 6 p.m., relieving on station and then shift to nighttime operations. Our operational area was the Long Tau and Soi Rap rivers. Patrolling the river approaches to Saigon was, to say the least, a mind game.

The Viet Cong continually studied the river boats operations to try and determine the patrol patterns of the boats. This in turn forced the river boat commanders to frequently change their mode of operation. "Charlie was smart and would use every trick he could think of to sneak by us," Townsend said. "We had to change our tactics nearly every night just to keep pace."

More than 30 years after he left Vietnam, Townsend who retired from the Navy as a lieutenant commander in June 1981, still speaks fondly of his tour in Vietnam and the men who volunteered to serve on the river boats.

"Here you saw Sailors at their finest from throughout the enlisted community. In my crews I had deck rates, aviation rates, gunner's mates... everything," Townsend said. "And, almost without exception they were all volunteers."

Although there was no such thing as a dull patrol, some were certainly more exciting than others. On one patrol, Townsend recalls with remorse, he and his crew were on night patrol when they came upon a sampan hugging the shoreline. Townsend illuminated the sampan and the four men aboard jumped into water.

"We threw them life preservers and tried to persuade them to surrender. Each time they would get alongside I would yell 'show me your hands, show me your hands.' They would hold up one hand but never both at the same time.

"When we would try to grab them they would dive. Finally, after what seemed like a lifetime and we couldn't get them to show us both hands at once, we shot them," Townsend said, choking back the emotion. "I didn't have any choice. The Viet Cong had used this same sort of tactic before to try and sink a patrol boat by tossing a hand grenade into the boat."

Although Chief Townsend and his boats conducted more than 200 combat patrols, boarded and searched hundreds of sampans and junks, confiscated thousands of pounds of enemy supplies and equipment, and repeatedly came under enemy fire, his crews managed to come through without a single loss of life. "That's the thing that I'm most proud of says the retired Brown Water river boat commander.

###

Joseph J. Quinn:

Out of Retirement

"Our primary job was dropping flares for the guys on the ground." That's how retired Marine Corps Master Gunnery Sergeant Joseph J. Quinn, recalls his main purpose for being in Vietnam. The Shell Point, South Carolina, native entered the war zone on Thanksgiving Day 1966.

Quinn had retired from the Marine Corps in 1961 after 20 years of active duty as an enlisted pilot and was working for the FAA, when he decided he wanted to go back on active duty. "I missed flying," he says, so I wrote the commandant (of the Marine Corps) a letter requesting a return to active duty in a flying status."

"I thought they'd send me somewhere like Cherry Point or El Toro to get me a few hours of flight time —but they sent me to Pendleton to get some 'physical refreshment.' When I checked into Pendleton they just wanted to know where I was staying and told me to check in every day or two and eventually they'd send me some orders."

A few weeks later he received orders for Chu Lai, South Vietnam, flying C-117s.

"And before you know it," he smiles, "I was re-qualified and flying my own plane as plane commander." Much of Quinn's flying in Vietnam was at night, at least twice a week he'd have to get airborne in the middle of the night. "They'd wake us up and say 'go man.' So we had just a few minutes to get in the airplane and go." Quinn and his crew saved many lives by doing so.

"We'd be talking with the squad leaders on the ground on the radio and they'd say 'keep dropping those flares just as long as you can.' "We would drop a flare every seven minutes or so from an altitude of about 5,000 feet. By keeping the light on the area at night the VC would stay off the troops. When daylight came, helicopters would go in and bring them out. Even though I was up there smoking cigars,

110

drinking coffee and dropping a flare once in a while, I guess it was appreciated.

"I'm surprised we didn't get more SAM hits, especially near the DMZ," he smiles.

Quinn says his other flying duties weren't quite as intense. "We'd occasionally take a USO troop from one base to another, or we'd fly PX supplies from one base to another, or do R&R passenger drops."

Quinn says he was very impressed with the "young grunts" he encountered in Vietnam.

"We'd bring them into Chu Lai, usually bringing them back from the hospital and they'd all have one or two Purple Hearts. I'd ask them why they wanted to go back with their outfits, and to a man they'd say the same thing. They just wanted to be with their guys. These were 18- and 19-year-old kids —just unbelievable. Certainly made me proud to be a Marine," Quinn says.

Quinn said his closest call during his Vietnam tour came on a stormy night en route to Okinawa in an R4D transport. He was flying as co-pilot that night with Master Sgt. Bob Lurie in the pilot's seat. They were taking 15 passengers, all Marines, to Kadena for R&R, when an engine went out.

Quinn and Lurie ordered all cargo and loose equipment off the plane, including personal baggage. The only thing they kept was their rifles and golf clubs. Thanks to the skill and experience of the two enlisted pilots, the flying sergeants safely landed the airplane and their fellow Marines at Kadena.

Quinn began his flying career in 1941, serving in the Virgin Islands as a rear-seater in an OS2-U patrol plane. "I was what you'd call a radioman/gunner," he reminisces. "In Korea," he continues, "I was a night fighter pilot in the F7F. That was a great airplane."

For his Korean service Quinn earned a Distinguished Flying Cross and three Air Medals. For his efforts in Vietnam, he earned several more Air Medals.

Quinn hung up his flight helmet for good in 1968 and returned to work with the FAA where he ultimately retired in 1983. "When I was working at the FAA (in the early 60s) there were a lot of people who were really against the war. Being an old military man that really rubbed me the wrong way," he says, "I guess maybe that's why I went back in. I have read an awful lot of books on Vietnam by various authors, and I've come to realize that it was a political war. Looking back on it," he muses, "I don't feel we were justified in being there. But at the same time, I glad I was able to do my part."

###

Robert K. Jones:

Last of the Navy Enlisted Pilots

When Master Chief Petty Officer Robert K. Jones retired from the Navy in 1983 he was the last of a breed—Navy enlisted pilots.

Master Chief Jones was awarded his Navy Wings of Gold as a naval aviation pilot in 1947 and during his more than 40 years of service, qualified in a total of 27 different aircraft— including seven jets.

In 1967, while most of his peers who had completed 20 years of service were retiring, Jones reported to the Naval Support Activity, Ton Son Nhut Air Base, South Vietnam, for duty as one of only four enlisted sea service pilots in Southeast Asia (the other three were Marines).

"We were basically a logistics outfit," Jones said "I flew an R4-D for the most part, on a regular route between Saigon and Da Nang, but occasionally I flew copilot in helicopters."

For aviators in Vietnam, enemy ground fire was a given but in at least one situation, Jones and his crew didn't realize they had been hit until their mission was complete and they were safely back on the ground.

"We dropped the landing gear in preparation for a landing at Binh Dinh," Jones recalls, and the hydraulic pressure wouldn't come back up. We made a routine landing and checked the system and found out that a 14mm round had come through the firewall and took a chuck of the hydraulic line out. Ironically, we didn't even know that we had been shot at."

On another occasion, Jones was flying co-pilot in a helicopter when the aircraft was downed by enemy fire.

"We had spent the entire day replenishing HAL-3, the Navy attack helicopter squadron, and were on our last hop of the day when NSA downtown (Naval Support Activity Saigon) asked us to deliver them some ammo. After picking up several cases of grenades, we were hovering over the NSA headquarters building when a sniper fired at us with a .50 caliber. A shall hit the tail rotor with just enough force to throw it out of balance.

"With the tail rotor out of action, the skipper managed to get the helicopter under control and land on the roof of the building. Thankfully that was the only time I was never shot down in Vietnam."

As an enlisted pilot during the Vietnam War, Jones was indeed a rare breed. Although more than 5,000 Navy, Marine Corps and Coast Guard enlisted men earned their wings between 1916 and 1948, most converted to officer status after World War II.

Jones said that despite the fact that he often flew with officers as his copilot that never presented a problem.

"On the ground that ensign or lieutenant junior grade out ranked me," Jones, said with a smile, "but in the air I was the boss and no one ever questioned that. That's just the way it is in aviation. The aircraft commander is always in charge, no matter what his rank is."

Like many senior naval aviators at the time, and Jones was a senior naval aviator based on the fact that he had more than 20 years aviation experience in a variety of aircraft, the master chief volunteered for duty in Vietnam. That seniority put him in the air the morning after he checked into NSA Saigon.

A Veteran of World War II and Korea, Jones said going to Vietnam was something he felt that he had to do.

"It was a decision I have never regretted," said Jones, "But on the other hand, I wasn't flying missions over Hanoi or Haiphong either."

While the master chief may not have been flying his aircraft in the path of SAM missiles over the North Vietnamese Capitol, his missions were no less dangerous.

"We were frequently fired at," Jones said, but generally it was from small arms and more often than not the people shooting at my plane were farmers.

"I remember this one time," Jones said, "we were rolling down the runway when a sniper appeared at the end of the runway. There was nothing I could do but apply power and hope to get airborne. As the airplane left the ground I kept waiting for something to happen... but it didn't. We found out later that the guy at the end of the runway was a farmer. The VC had given him a shotgun and told him to shoot at American airplanes as they took off. What he actually done was stand there and shoot into the air," Jones laughed.

At the time of his retirement in 1981, as the Navy's last enlisted pilot, Master Chief Petty Officer Robert Jones was assigned to the Pensacola (Florida) Naval Air Station as a C-131 pilot.

###

Ray Cwikowski:

<u>362 Days in Happy Valley</u>

Phan Rang Air Base wasn't exactly paradise, and retired Air Force Lieutenant Colonel Ray Cwikowski (see-kowski) isn't exactly Colonel Potter from the hit television series "M.A.S.H.," but the similarities are worth noting.

Then Captain Cwikowski commanded the 35th Transportation Squadron at Phan Rang —affectionately termed "Happy Valley."

"I didn't want to be there —I didn't know what the hell I was doing," he smiles. "I was there because of a change in my specialty code." Cwikowski says his area of expertise was in air transportation. He was sent to Southeast Asia as a motor vehicle maintenance officer.

"I had a top-secret clearance, crypto, category II extra-sensitive information," he continues. "According to the book, I should never have been sent overseas —or anywhere near enemy territory."

Cwikowski arrived at Phan Rang in a C-130. "I sat on my luggage. Real uncomfortable," he smiled. "Its pitch black with stormy weather," he continues. "We land at the base they open the back ramp with the engines running and yell at me to 'get out! Get out now!' We don't want to stay and get hit.' The base was on one side of the airfield, my office on the other.

"When I reached my office there was a guy sitting there with a bottle of Jack Daniels. He looks at me and says, 'Howdy there captain, what can we do for you?' He didn't realize he was talking to his new commander."

In Vietnam just three days shy of a year, Cwikowski accumulated enough "war stories" to keep both his and the neighborhood grandchildren's attention for years.

"The 7th Air Force called us one night and wanted us to run a convoy to Cam Rahn Bay (45 miles to the north) to pick up bombs. They asked me if I knew the 7th Air Force people were under attack. I could see the tracers coming in from the back gate, so there was nothing really between me and the tracers." As if that wasn't scary enough, Cwikowski recalls another exciting night.

"One night I dropped someone off at the airport on the other side of the base. We had this perimeter road that came around the airfield to the main base." (Cwikowski was in a jeep with canvas top on it.)

"The perimeter was ringed with watchtowers and guys with machine guns, and surrounded by barbed wire equipped with trip flares (flares went off when touched, allowing personnel to fire at the area of flash).

"So as I'm driving around the perimeter road, I hear these staccato bursts going off. I figure I'm being shot at so I'm driving like hell with my head ducking. After a few horrifying minutes I realized it was the canvas flap on the jeep making the noise."

One other time, three sergeants and I were coming down from Cam Rahn Bay. I was driving. Here I was looking like General Patton —helmet, flak vest, goggles sandbags on the floor in case of land mines —and we get this flat tire.

We were just five miles from the back gate of Happy Valley so we lock and load. As one of the guys is changing the tire dust starts flying up. We're being shot at.

"We got the tire on with just a couple of lug nuts and got the hell out of there. It turns out that the snipers are Korean soldiers, supposedly American Allies, just trying to be funny,"

Ironically, Cwikowski says he actually had more problems with Korean soldiers than he had with the North Vietnamese.

"The Koreans were paid the same scale as American soldiers," Cwikowski said. "It was big money for them. But their R&R (rest and recreation time) was based on body count and their body count often included old men, women, and kids. We'd say, 'what the hell are you doing here?' They'd point to the bodies and say "Viet Cong, Viet Cong.' We'd say, 'so where are their weapons?'

"I even had one Korean officer pull a gun on one of my men in the Post Exchange over the purchase of a stereo unit. It was the last stereo they had and the Korean officer apparently wanted it very badly. They were always stealing stuff from us.

"And then there was the kimchee to deal with. The Koreans were actually supplied with canned kimchee by a supply contractor in Hawaii. Kimchee, if you're not familiar with it, is basically rotten cabbage— stinks to high heaven. Wow! Their (Koreans) breath could really kill you when they got up close and started talking to you."

Cwikowski said what bothered him most in Vietnam, however, wasn't his Korean Allies— but the attitude of many of his fellow officers.

"The wing commanders, the base commanders, a lot of them felt we had no business being there. I was somewhat disillusioned. I wondered how we were supposed to get the job done if the senior officers felt that way."

"When you're in command of 118 men, as I was, you have to believe in what you're doing. That's real important. But now that some time has passed and I've had time to think about it, I didn't think we should have been there either. It was a civil war— we had no business sticking our face in there."

Duty in Vietnam for Cwikowski wasn't all-bad. It also had its high points. One in particular was being able to meet motion picture star, Raquel Welch, who was in Vietnam as part of the 1967 Bob Hope USO Christmas show — Operation Holly.

For routine entertainment, Cwikowski and his men frequently listened to Hanoi Hannah. "She had the best newscast, in Southeast Asia" he laughs. "Oh, she talked a lot about the protests back home, but we never really paid much attention to the war protest. When we were there (Vietnam) what was going on in the States was relatively unimportant. Our primary focus was staying alive so we could return to the States." said Cwikowski.

Like many other officers who served in Vietnam, Cwikowski says he wasn't particularly a big fan of General William C. Westmoreland, former commander of U.S. forces in Vietnam. "We called him the 'Boy Scout,' said Cwikowski because he wanted to run the war like a Boy Scout troop. I remember one of the visits he made to our base. Not once did he complement the men on what they had accomplished, instead, he complained that the buses were running off the side of the road and dragging mud onto the highway and that grass was growing out of the sand bags on top of the bunkers. How can you expect to win a war with that kind of leadership?

But what really frustrated me was seeing people getting killed in noncombat situations. It happened all the time and there was no good reason for it. I remember on one occasion, I had to put everybody in trenches around the barracks. All we had were three clips of ammunition per man —54 rounds each— that was it. Worse still, the Air Force didn't train it's airmen for ground combat. So all of a sudden here you have 118 guys in trenches with guns thinking that they're about to be overrun. All the time I'm praying... please guys, don't shoot each other. It was that sort of thing that made you wonder if we were ever really prepared for something like Vietnam."

###

John B. (J.B.) McKamey:

<u>Seven Years in the Hanoi Hilton</u>

In the summer of 1965, John B. (J.B.) McKamey, was a cocky, young A-4E pilot, with Attack Squadron 23 (VA-23) flying combat missions from the USS Midway (CVA-41).

One sunny day in June 1965, McKamey and his wingman were assigned to fly a routine reconnaissance flight over North Vietnam. After an hour or so of what appeared to be an uneventful flight, the VA-23 pilots headed back toward the Midway. Outbound at around 5,000 feet, the A- 4s crossed over a river.

Carefully observing the scene below, the young lieutenant saw what appeared to be pylons extending about a quarter of the way out into the river. Believing that he had located a construction site, McKamey radioed his wingman that he was dropping down for a closer look.

"I had bottomed out at 1,200 feet," said McKamey, "when suddenly I heard a sharp "thump, thump! —not unlike a knock on a door —on the side of the aircraft and I immediately lost all electrical power. I recalled an earlier debriefing when another VA-23 pilot told of encountering a similar incident and still managed to get back to the ship by engaging the emergency generator, which dropped down into the wind stream to generate power... so I wasn't too worried," McKamey said.

"I put the plane into a climb and reached for the generator. I jerked the handle, and it came off in my hand. That's when I began to realize that I was probably in more trouble then I realized."

As McKamey fought for altitude, the cockpit of his A-4E Skyhawk filled with smoke. Guessing that he was at an altitude of about 5,000 feet and flying level, he ejected.

Nearly eight years later during a chance meeting with his former wing man at the Alameda, Calif., Naval Air Station Officers' Club, McKamey learned that his A-4E had been engulfed in flames when he ejected. And, although the pilot had seen McKamey's parachute open, he lost sight of him as soon as he hit the ground. McKamey's fate remained unknown for nearly four years.

As his parachute drifted toward earth, McKamey saw that he was going to land in an open area. "As I watched the ground come up I tried to recall what I had learned in survival training," he said.

"But all I could think of were scenes from old World War II movies in which downed flyers always made an issue of hiding their parachutes,'' McKamey said with a laugh.

As he recovered the chute, which had draped over a small ditch, he saw a number of armed, black-clad Vietnamese running toward him shouting. With no cover in sight and armed only with a .38-caliber pistol, loaded with tracer rounds, he was quickly apprehended.

"I was taken prisoner and after walking for about five hours, put in a small prison near Hue. I was confined there for about 10 days while awaiting transportation to Hanoi. You have to remember," McKamey said, "that during this time in the war, there was an awfully lot of traffic moving south, but hardly anything going north. Finally, an officer and four guards in a jeep picked me up and we started a two-and-a-half day trip to Hanoi. At first we traveled only at night. But as we got closer to the capital, we drove a few hours during daylight.

"Arriving in Hanoi, I was put into a solitary cell in Hoa Lo Prison— the infamous 'Hanoi Hilton.' Then after about 30 minutes, I was moved to another cell. During the move I heard an obvious American voice ask my name and whether I was Air Force or Navy.

That was the last American voice I heard for a long time. But the fact that someone knew I was there made me feel better... even if that someone was another prisoner.

After being placed in the second cell, an English speaking North Vietnamese officer came in. Upon being questioned, McKamey responded in accordance with the Code of Conduct by giving his rank, name, date of birth and service number.

When he refused to answer any other questions, McKamey's hands were placed behind his back; palms turned outward, and manacles placed on his wrists.

A rope was tied tightly above the elbows, looped around his neck, pulled between his legs and secured to the manacles. The interrogation continued.

"What type aircraft were you flying? What is your ship? What was your mission?"

"My name is John B. McKamey. Lieutenant junior grade, U.S. Navy. Date of bir...."

The guard pulled the rope tighter; forcing McKamey's shoulders back in an unnatural position, nearly pulling them out of joint. His manacled hands were then placed on a small stool and the guard jumped up and down on the manacles, forcing them ever tighter and causing metal to cut into his flesh.

At this point the lieutenant blacked out. "The pain was so bad that I lost all track of time," said McKamey. "It may have only been a few minutes, but it seemed like hours. I really don't know.

"Finally, I said, 'OK! I'll write whatever you want me to write. That was the only sensible thing to do. You hold out as long as you can, but while you still have the capacity to think clearly, you had to give them something to keep them off your back so that you can get a little rest."

McKamey said he feels that most, if not all, Vietnam POWs would agree that it was better to give their captors some sort of gibberish rather than hold out until you were broken and then perhaps give them something they could use for propaganda purposes.

"There was just no sensible reason to resist to the point of death," he continued.

McKamey said that because he was captured so early in the war he wasn't punished or interrogated nearly as harshly as those Americans captured later.

"In 1965 Americans were still somewhat of a novelty to the North Vietnamese and POWs were fairly well treated and actually better fed than their guards, McKamey said.

"When I was taken prisoner, they actually went to a nearby French restaurant and bought our food. There wasn't much of it, but it was good," said McKamey. "On the Fourth of July 1966, the special meals ended. They changed our diet from French to Vietnamese food. Although the quality went down by about 50 percent, the quantity went up by about 50 percent. Actually, it was a pretty good trade. When you're really hungry, taste isn't that much of a consideration."

Over the next four years, according to the retired A-4E pilot, both the quality and quantity steadily decreased and the POWs started losing weight. Withholding of food was a favorite means of punishment.

After being in captivity for about 30 days, a U.S. Air Force major was moved into a cell about three cells away. "At that time he was the senior POW and they were kind of rough on him," recalls McKamey. "For one thing they stopped feeding him. But we had a common bath area, so one day I yelled out the window and told him to look in a certain place in the bath area for food. When I received my food, I would hide part of it and take it to the bath area. There I would re-hide what little food I could for the major to retrieve later when he went to the bath area. Going to the bath, was one of the few things he was allowed to do."

In describing his more than seven years as a POW in Vietnam, McKamey said the sheer boredom was one of the worst things that he and his fellow POWs had to contend with.

"There was absolutely nothing to do. We just sat in our cells day in, day out."

Beginning sometime in 1969, four years after his capture, things begin to take a turn for the better.

For the first time he was allowed to write home. The prisoners were allowed out of their cells for exercise periods and the food started to improve.

"I'm not sure what caused the changes," McKamey said. "There were a number of things happening. Peace talks were under way in Paris; the American people had started a massive letter-writing campaign, flooding the North Vietnamese embassy in Paris with thousands of letters weekly— and Ho Chi Minh died."

In January 1972, all of the POWs from camps surrounding Hanoi were brought to the Hanoi Hilton and addressed by the camp commander in accordance with the Paris Accords. The American POWs were told they were to be gradually released in the order of their capture. Soon after, McKamey returned home. It had been seven years and eight months since that fatal day when he was launched from the deck of the USS Midway for what he thought would be just another routine reconnaissance mission.

McKamey retired from the Navy in 1986 as a Navy captain and was among the first Vietnam POWs to receive the POW Medal when the medal was authorized in 1989.

###

Ross Randle Terry:

POW Recalls Day
<u>His Life Went On Hold</u>

For many Americans, the Vietnam War was, and is, considered one of the darkest periods in American history. But for those who were there, particularly those who had the misfortune of being incarcerated by the North Vietnamese, the war in Southeast Asia robbed them of a big slice of their lives. The day they were detained as POWs is the day their life went on hold. Retired Navy Captain Ross Randle Terry is one of those former POWs.

Terry, then a lieutenant, was flying in F-4 Phantoms as a Radar Intercept Officer with VF-154 deployed aboard the USS Coral Sea (CV-43). Terry and his pilot, Lieutenant Commander Neils Tanner were only mildly apprehensive as they relaxed in the VF-154 ready room and listened to the briefing officer detail their planned strike on the railroad yards at Phu Ly, some 20 miles south of Hanoi. Terry and Tanner were assigned the task of flak suppression. Their mission was to take out an 85mm flak site, a ring of 85mm anti-aircraft guns around the rail yard, thus lessening the danger to the attack aircraft as they made their bombing runs on the yard. When the ship's meteorologist stepped forward to give his portion of the briefing, he merely confirmed what the airmen already knew. Yankee Station (the Seventh Fleet's operating area in the Gulf of Tokin) and most of North Vietnam was under a heavy overcast that Sunday October 9, 1966.

The briefing over, Terry and Neils, as they had done dozens of times before, climbed in their F-4 and prepared for launch. They fully expected to be back on board Coral Sea in plenty of time for the evening moving in the wardroom. Tanner gave a thumbs-up to the catapult officer and a few seconds later, the F-4 was propelled off the flight deck into the overcast skies of the Gulf of Tonkin. The drop of the "cat" officer's arm performed a double function that cloudy October Sunday. It signaled the launch of Terry and Tanner's F-4 Phantom and put life, as they had known it, on hold for seven years.

"We broke through the overcast and dove on the target," Terry recalls. "Just as we released our bombs we felt a 'thump' in the mid-section of the aircraft. Neils pulled off, fired off the afterburner and tried to make it to Laos. Neils and I had agreed earlier that if we should be hit we would try for Laos rather than fly over a very heavily fortified bridge in an attempt to make it back to the gulf. The Golden BB (flak) destroyed our hydraulics causing Neils to lose control of the aircraft. The plane pitched upward, rolled and went into about a 135-degree bank with a 60-degree nose down angle. Our speed was around mock 1.3 when I ejected."

At that angle and speed, the force of the ejection was so great that the pressure stripped the helmet, oxygen mask and most of the survival gear from Terry's body and tore three panels from his parachute. Ironically, the Sugarland, Texas, native credits the damaged chute with saving his life. "There must have been at least a 1,000 people on the ground, many of them shooting at me. The missing panels caused my descent to be much faster than it normally would have been, causing those people shooting at me to miss." Terry said he believes that many American airmen were killed that way.

"I hit the ground and was immediately surrounded by a swarm of North Vietnamese civilians shouting and waving guns, clubs and knifes. I remember this one guy ran up and was about to cut my throat," the captain said, gently rubbing a finger over a still visible scar on his neck, "when two military guys fired their AK-47s over the crowd's head. The knife-wielding civilian backed off. Remembering what we had been told I fished out my Geneva Convention card and tried to give it to the soldiers. They took the card, cut it into pieces and threw it on the ground. My shoes were then taken away, I was stripped down to my shorts and led through a little outlying village and put in a cave. People then lined up and filed past to get a look at this tall, white, red-haired guy. I sort of felt like something in a zoo," Terry recalls. "These people hated us. Even though they had never seen an American before, Ho Chi Minh had kept them worked up. They really believed that we were war mongers who had come to kill them."

A short time after being put in the cave, Terry was visited by an English speaking interpreter who demanded to know not only his name, rank and service number but what type of aircraft he was flying, what ship he had flown from and how was he shot down. Terry, in accordance with the Geneva Convention and the Code of Conduct gave only his name, rank, service number and date of birth.

When it became obvious to his captors that they would get no further information from the lanky, red-haired American flyer, they tied him up by the elbows and dragged him around the cave. "At this point of my capture," said Terry, "I was mostly sacred. I didn't know that to expect.

"The pain hadn't really set in yet because of the newness of where I was and what was going on. That evening, they took me through another crowd, dragged me up on a make-shift stage and beat me down on my knees to the delight of the screaming crowd.

"Kneeling there on my knees, my hands tied behind my back, I noticed this one guy standing at the edge of the crowd. He stood out by the fact he wasn't taking part in the screaming and clapping. He was also holding a three-foot sword. I thought 'man that guy is going to try and kill me.' The crowd worked itself into a frenzy, so to protect me; the guards grabbed me and tossed me into the back of a truck. The truck had bamboo slats around the bed and I remember leaning against them when I had this strange feeling that something was about the happen. It was like a little voice telling me to fall down and roll to the middle of the truck bed. Just as I dropped, the quite man with the sword drove it through the bamboo slats, just where I had been standing."

Leaving the village, Terry and his captors traveled most of the night and around 5 a.m. arrived at "Heart Break Hotel," one of several prison compounds in the Hanoi area. There he was put in shackles and the interrogation and torture started up again. "What is the name of your ship? What kind of aircraft do you fly? What was your target? How many airplanes do you have on your ship? How were you shot down?"

After about eight hours of continuous torture, Terry told his interrogators that he had been shot down by a MiG. "After that amount of time you're hurting enough that you began to rationalize. Maybe if you can give them some worthless information you can get them off of your back for a little while. The story about being shot down by a MiG was apparently what they wanted to hear because the beating stopped.

"Even though I had a brief reprieve I didn't feel a whole lot better. By telling them that I had been shot down by a MiG, in my mind, I had gone beyond name, rank, service number and date of birth. At that point in time I really felt that I had somehow betrayed the code and I was the only one to have done such a thing.

"I was then taken to a little room with stocks in it. They put one leg in the stocks, handcuffed me and put my arms in another set of stocks so that I was in a bent-up position. After a few days and nights like that, it begins to get your attention. And you start to wonder how long you can hold out if they want something more from you. Sure enough, after awhile they were back. Fortunately, a voice from the other side of the room called out, 'Don't let them permanently injure you. Just fight the best you can.'"

Terry knew then, that he was not alone and wasn't the only person to fabricate a story for the North Vietnamese, so he stuck to his MiG story. After a few more days he was reunited with Lieutenant Commander Tanner and transferred to "the Zoo." The Zoo, according to Terry, was a former French motion picture studio, which had been converted into a cellblock. During its heyday as a movie studio, the cells had been used for film storage. Vents were used to keep a steady flow of air flowing through the small rooms, therefore keeping the film at a fairly constant temperature. The Vietnamese had long since plugged up the vents, turning the former lockers into ovens. As a result of having their hands shackled for so long, neither Terry nor Tanner was able to use their hands. Still they helped one another as best they could.

By now the two VF-154 flyers had been confined long enough to learn the tap code — a modified form of Morris Code the POWs used to communicate — and day-by-day learned a little more about their surroundings and who some of their fellow POWs were. They also learned that the Vietnamese used whatever information, true or otherwise, they could extract from them for propaganda purposes.

As the days, weeks and months went by, more and more pressure was applied to try and pry information from Terry, Tanner and the other POWs at the Zoo. Often, under the threat of death, they were forced to write, or dictate "confessions." One of those "confessions" made it to the Paris peace talks and bought Terry and Tanner a severe beating and months of solitary confinement.

"It's not something I would necessary recommend to a future POW," said Terry, "but Neils and I dreamed up what we called the 'Clark Kent & Ben Casey Caper'. We decided to 'confess.' Our hands were still in such bad shape that neither of us could write, so we dedicated our 'confessions.' I was Clark Kent and Neils was Ben Casey (fictional television characters). According to our confessions, Kent was supposedly a Navy lieutenant flying off of a carrier. He had become disenchanted with American policy and said the war was immoral and illegal and he was therefore turning in his wings.

Casey, also a Navy flyer, was supposedly being divorced by his wife because of his involvement in the Vietnam War. The guard wrote down everything just the way we told it to him; buzz words and all. It was later shipped off to Paris where peace talks between the United States and North Vietnam were taking place. For about two months after the 'confession' they pretty much left us alone. By that I mean we weren't beat as often.

"The so-called confession was later read to the international press by an Englishman named Bertrand Russell who was conducting a so-called 'war crimes tribunal.' Well as soon as the press heard the names Clark Kent and Ben Casey, they stampeded for the telephones. That of course gave Russell and his tribunal, as well as the North Vietnamese government, a black eye.

As soon as the word got back to where we were at, there were a lot of sudden changes at the Zoo. Interrogators were changed, guards were transferred, and Neils and I got the hell beat of us. Neils was sent to another prison called Alcatraz and I was put in a little place called the Outhouse. For the next six months or so we sit in solitary in stocks and cuffs."

After the stocks and cuffs were finally removed, Terry remained in solitary for another 18 months. While living alone, he managed to make a couple of new friends with whom he passed the time of day. His friends were named "Myself" and "I" Captain Terry recalls that during those 18 months he, Myself and I, designed and built houses, played cards and in general searched for ways to keep from going insane. "The guards would hear me talking to myself and put a finger to their heads and make circular motions, to indicate that I had gone crazy."

During his years as a prisoner of war, Terry said he and his fellow Vietnam POWs lived under extremely harsh conditions. Their lives were continually threatened and they were frequently beaten and tortured. But intermixed with the harshness and brutally were also moments of kindness and compassion. "I remember one Christmas," Terry recalls, "when the Rabbit (a guard so nicknamed because of his ears) brought me in for a quiz and held a picture of a lady and five young girls up in front of me. I knew I had four girls but not five. Susan (Terry's wife) was about two month's pageant when I deployed and the baby was born after I was shot down. That, of course, was a very welcome Christmas present."

Terry was allowed to keep the family picture, which had come in a letter, but he wasn't as lucky with other packages from home, particularly those containing food. "As our time in captive stretched out, mail and packages came more frequently. But packages with food in them were usually confiscated by the guards."

Compassion, of sorts, was also shown in other ways. Terry recalls one occasion, when his wrists were sore and bleeding from being tightly shackled for a long period of time. "This guard came in with a bowl of rice. He uncuffed one hand, as they usually did, so that I could eat.

When I was finished, he put the cuffs back on my wrist and there was only one 'click'. At first I thought he had just made a mistake. He looked at me, placed a finger to his lips, in a gesture to be quiet, turned and walked away." After a good night's sleep, the first in a long time without his hands being cuffed behind him, Terry became concerned about the guard and re-secured the handcuffs himself.

On yet another occasion, when Terry had been beaten and forced to sit in a kneeling position with his hands shackled behind him, a guard brought him a boiled potato, concealed in a tin can, and fed it to him. Afterward, the guard lit a cigarette and held it to Terry's lips so that he could have a few puffs. Terry said he never saw that particular guard again.

Eventually Terry was moved from solitary to a two-man cell. "That required some adjustment," the captain explains. "After nearly two years in solitary, I hardly knew how to talk to another human being. I was then moved to what was called the Zoo Annex—another part of the former studio—with six other guys." The annex had six rooms with six men to each room. This was the first time since he was shot down that the red-haired Texan had seen so many Americans at one time. With that many American POWs together it was inevitable that sooner or later an escape attempt would be made. Through their crude, but effective communication system an escape plan was devised. It was decided the escape would take place on a rainy night because the guards generally stayed inside during bad weather. One stormy night as the rain beat down, two POWs, both Air Force officers, managed to get out of their cell and over an outer wall. Within hours, however, they were recaptured and returned to the Zoo where they were brutally beaten and tortured until one of the escapees died.

Terry, the annex's senior ranking officer and the senior officer from each room was then put through what he refers to as "18 days of hell."

"We were laterally beaten and tortured for 18 days. They would set you in a chair, all tied up, on the top of a table and leave you there until you fell asleep and fell off the table. The fall of course would cause still more pain and sometimes broken bones. Another favorite tactic was to strip you down and beat you across the buttocks with a fan belt until you were bleeding. Another thing they would do, is hold your legs out and strike you in about three places across the shins with a piece of bamboo until your legs began to swell up and then whack then again. That really gets your attention. All the time they are beating you they are trying to get you to tell them who ordered the escape.

"It's one thing to say something that you know is baloney and you know that the country knows it's baloney (such as the Clark Kent and Ben Casey caper), but it's something entirely different to say something against a man they have their hands on," Terry explains. "Finally the beatings ended and they chained me to Colonel Bob Purcell. We were cuffed and manacled together and put in a room with three other 'couples' so to speak. We stayed that way for about three months."

After North Vietnam President Ho Chi Minh died Terry and many of his fellow POWs, were moved to a new prison at Son Tay, a few miles northwest of Hanoi. Unbeknown to the POWs, American Special Forces were making plans to raid Son Tay in an attempt to rescue them. Unfortunately North Vietnamese intelligence found out about the attempt and moved them, just hours, before the Americans arrived. The Son Tay prisoners were relocated and put in large 50-man cells.

As the war begin to wind down, the torture and beatings became less frequent and Terry and his fellow POWs were allowed more time outside and given better food. They begin to hear rumors that the war was about over and they would soon be going home. On several occasions, some of his cellmates were actually told they were going to leave, only to be turned back at the last minute. But finally the day of repatriation did arrive and the freedom birds began to arrive in Hanoi.

In March 1973, Capt. Terry and his squadron mate, Neils Tanner, were flown to Clark Air Force Base in the Philippines and finally to Naval Air Station Memphis, Tenn., where they were hospitalized for more than three months.

On Sept. 21, 1990, seventeen-and-a-half years after leaving Vietnam, Captain Ross Randle Terry was awarded the POW Medal.

###

Norman E. Schrader:

Seawolfs of the Mekong

Norman E. Schrader wanted to be a warrior. He wanted go to Vietnam and at the height of the war, he got his wish.

Schrader had joined the Navy in 1956 and during boot camp was selected for the Naval Aviation Cadet program. I was accepted for flight school and received my wings in 1958."

By the mid-'60s he'd had several assignments and the war in Vietnam was well underway.

In 1968, he volunteered for duty with the Navy's only gunship squadron, Helicopter Attack Squadron (Light) Three, HAL-3—the Seawolves. He arrived in Vietnam at the end of the Tet Offensive.

"The first impression I had of Vietnam was how hot it was; and that I would actually be handling guns and rockets, and shooting at people," he said. "But that's what I'd been training for and that's what we were there for."

The squadron's primary job was to provide support for river patrol boats and other units, including the Navy's elite special operations force, the SEALs. "We would drop anything we were doing to provide cover for our guys," he said. "We did what had to be done to help them out.

"The Army was initially tasked with providing that support but the Navy because, of its night and all-weather missions, decided that they needed to get some of their own pilots and aircraft over there," says Schrader." But the Army still supported the riverine operations of Task Force 117. One day the Army came up short on gunships and my fire team was sent in to provide support for Task Force 117.

"Task Force 117 came under attack and we found ourselves smack in the middle of it. In the midst of the battle, there were several radios all crackling messages at the same time. A couple of the voices directing mobile riverine force traffic sounded awful familiar.

They were the voices of a former commodore of mine and his chief staff officer.

"We had been laying down a lot of fire on the bad guys and needed to re-arm," Schrader said. "There was a re-arming facility about 10 minutes away. I got on the radio and told the riverine force traffic controller that we'd be back in a few minutes. The commodore got on the radio and asked who I was and where I was going. I told him my name and told him I were I was going.

"A short time later, I'm still sitting in my helicopter at the re-arming facility, when these two senior officers come over to my helo. Suddenly here the three us are out on the tarmac hugging each other. That was one of the most interesting things that happened to me during my tour in Vietnam," said Schrader."

When not supporting the PBRs, Schrader and his detachment, Det-5 would go on patrols. "We were always within easy striking distance of known bad guys," he said. There were a lot of genuine heroes in that squadron, but the guys I was most impressed with were the door gunners. Those guys literally hung out on the skids of the helicopter to keep fire trained on the bad guys when the helos were in vulnerable positions. A lot of us wouldn't be here if not for them," he said.

Another incident Schrader recalls, is the time HAL-3 was operating from a huge yard vessel, near Chau Doc. His fire team was scrambled to intercept a large number of suspected Viet Cong boats coming in from Cambodia.

When Schrader and his team arrived on scene, they found a flotilla of junks and sampans of various sizes, some with 10 people, some with 20-30 people. "Intelligence told us exactly where they'd be and they were. But something just didn't seem right to me. I had my wingman remain at altitude to cover the operation while I took my helicopter down to a low hover close aboard the sampans for a close inspection. Although the door gunners had weapons trained on the sampans, we decided after observing the actions of these people they were not the enemy."

I had the gunners attempt to elicit a hostile response by firing near the sampans. There was no hostile response, just obvious fear. I decided at that time that they were not the enemy and we were going to leave them alone. Intelligence later revealed the people in the sampans were South Vietnamese returning to their homes.

Schrader left Vietnam the first time in the spring of 1969.

In 1972, while assigned to Helicopter Antisubmarine squadron Seven (HS-7), at Quonset Point, Rhode Island, he found out that he would be returning to Vietnam. "We were flying down to Mayport, Florida, when we received a message from NAS Norfolk to land there.

"We were told the carrier USS Saratoga had been diverted from a six-month Mediterranean deployment for a yearlong tour with Seventh Fleet in the Gulf of Tonkin.

"Additional helicopter pilots were needed onboard Saratoga and some members from HS-7 were tagged to go. We were trained as an eight-plane antisubmarine warfare squadron; but we quickly changed to a four-plane combat support squadron.

"Almost everyone in the squadron wanted to go, but couldn't," he said. "The toughest chore we had was telling people they couldn't go to Vietnam."

HS-7's mission during that deployment was to provide combat support for aircraft operating from the Saratoga and other Seventh Fleet units. Schrader left Vietnam for the second time in December 1972 and retired from the Navy in 1977.

###

William R. Smith:

Disaster on Yankee Station

"One of the things I remember most was the smell. There's no other smell like burned flesh," recalls retired Navy photographer William R. Smith.

The odor of horror Smith recalled was from burned bodies onboard the USS Forrestal (CVA-59) on July 29, 1967.

That day on Yankee Station off the coast of Vietnam a Zuni rocket was accidentally fired from an F-4 Phantom into the fuel pod of an A-4 Skyhawk on Forrestal's deck.

According to Smith, "It was exactly 10:52 a.m. when "all hell broke loose. I was in the operational intelligence center lab processing film. Up on the flight deck fuel and fire from a 400-gallon pod spread quickly. A 1,000 pound bomb fell off the A-4 and it didn't take long for it to cook off," he said. "I thought we were under attack. We were on the O-3 level right under the flight deck."

To exacerbate the problem, the deck of the Forrestal was loaded with planes readying for launch, all filled with fuel and ammunition and carrying armed rockets and bombs.

There were many secondary explosions. "There was enough stuff on those planes to blow up half of Vietnam," Smith recalls

"A lieutenant commander and I dove under a table," he said. "There was an ensign who walked by in a daze. He didn't know what was going on any more than the man in the moon. We grabbed one of his legs and pulled him under the table with us. There was debris falling all around us. The fire and explosions stopped just short of us."

Under fire call and general quarters, Smith followed procedure and grabbed his cameras. "We had what we called 'ready cameras,' loaded with film and ready to shoot. We ran up to the flight deck and started shooting. Photographing anything that walked, crawled or creeped."

Smith and his fellow photo mates recorded the horrific event on film for the first hour that the fires were being fought. "I don't know how much film we shot, there's no telling. We figured we couldn't shoot too much."

After that first hour Smith went to work on the fires. Fuel and bombs had fallen into holes caused by the initial explosions.

"The initial damage control party was exhausted and they needed relief." Smith had been a boatswain's mate before becoming a photographer and told his boss if there were enough photographers, he would go help fight the fires.

"I went and cooled bulkheads for a couple of hours until I was relieved," he said. "No one was merely a photographer, or a cook, or supply man that day—we were all sailors—fighting to save our ship.

"I saw one guy run into a compartment where a shipmate was screaming. He took a deep breath, went in and pulled something off the other guy, who had been trapped, and carried him out at the risk of his own life. I didn't know either one of them and never did learn their names. But I'll never forget the heroism of that sailor who... at the risk of his own life... went to aid a trapped shipmate.

"Two Marines went into a compartment filled with chlorine gas and gave their lives trying to save some guys trapped in there," he explained.

"We really weren't worried about the fire in itself," explained Smith. "We were worried about heat on the bombs, fuel, ammo, rockets and pyrotechnics below decks. And, of course, the nukes that possibly were onboard. We were never told that the Forrestal actually carried nuclear weapons. But it's a good assumption that we did.

"We ran interference between the bomb lockers and the fire," he said. "We worked our way out from the lockers to keep ourselves from blowing up."

When not helping with fire fighting and damage control, the Forrestal's photographers were doing their jobs. "We got an awful lot of dirty looks with us shooting pictures while guys were dying all over the place. But we were only doing our job, and most of the guys understood that. But at the time there were some sailors who didn't care for what we were doing. They thought we were just being insensitive.

Smith says that in his opinion, the real hero of the day was the Forrestal's commanding officer Captain John K. Beling. "He immediately turned the ship into the wind, kicked the speed up and blew that mess aft. If he'd not done that, I believe the Forrestal would have sunk.

"I saw so many young men grow up instantly that day—little guys, weighing no more than 120 pounds throwing bombs over the side that weighed twice as much as they did. Officers, chiefs and white hats working side by side—with only one goal in mind, save the ship. By evening we had the fire out and many of the men who were wounded were transferred to the USS Repose and USS Oriskany (a similar fate had struck Oriskany a year earlier—October 26, 1966— killing 44 Sailors).

That night Smith said everyone was mentally and physically exhausted, and scared. "I started thinking about my wife because she would certainly hear about the tragedy and wouldn't know immediately if I were alive or not. I thought about my kids and how I wanted to be able to tell them what happened.

"Then we got word we could send one short message," he said. "I sent my wife a telegram that said 'Am fine. Letter follows.'

"I'll never forget that day," Smith says. "I doubt that any of us will ever forget, the bodies stacked up in the hangar bay like cordwood until they could be refrigerated. Even today I can go aboard Forrestal and still smell that odor—the odor of death," he says.

"Tons of paint have been put on that ship since the fire but the odor is still there. The odor of ash, cinder, flesh, hair—the combination of all those—you can smell it. Any veteran of that ill-fated deployment can go onboard and smell it. For years afterward, and probably still today, veterans of that cruise who go onboard the carrier, walk around the area where the bodies of our shipmates were stacked," said Smith, choking back tears. "They won't walk over that area; they walk around it out of respect.

"Being a Navy photographer, even before the disaster on Yankee Station, I had seen and photographed death," says Smith, now an ordained minister in Pensacola, Florida, "but I saw more death that day than ever before or since. I pray that I never see anything like that again."

The photographs and motion pictures footage shot that day by Smith and the other Forrestal photographers have been used for years to help train sailors in shipboard safety and firefighting.

###

Ronald David:

Five O'clock Follies

No story about Vietnam would be complete without mentioning the infamous "Five O'clock Follies." the daily press briefings held by the Military Assistance Command Vietnam (MACV) Public Affairs Office.

The idea was to provide reporters with daily information about combat and other military operations, which had occurred in the past 24 hours.

However, due to the necessity of maintaining military secrecy the briefings didn't always provide the answers the media in Vietnam were looking for. On other occasions briefing officers would decline to confirm something because they didn't have the latest information. This led to an adversarial relationship between MACV and the media.

One of those briefing officers is retired Army Colonel Ronald "Ron" David. David was on his second Vietnam tour when he was tagged for the MACV public affairs assignment. The colonel initially went to Vietnam as a helicopter pilot with the 1st Cavalry Air Mobile Division in August 1965. After 11 months in country he was reassigned to a duty station in Europe.

"I actually thought I could get lost in Europe and never have to worry about another Vietnam tour," David said. But after 18 months or so in Europe, the Army decided that it needed CH-47 Chinook helicopter pilots in Vietnam. David, a major at the time, was one of eight UH-1 Huey gunship pilots tagged to be retained as a CH-47 pilot.

"There was no way in hell that I wanted to fly Chinooks," said David. "If I had to go back to Vietnam, I wanted to go back and fly a Cobra gunship. The Cobra was just entering service with the Army. I found another major with the same background and qualifications as I had, who wanted to fly Chinooks. So I tried to arrange a swap, but the Army said no. Chinook pilots were needed more than gunship pilots."

Within a matter of weeks, David found himself at Fort Rucker, Alabama, learning how to fly the huge CH-47. After qualifying in the Chinook, David returned to Vietnam in March 1968. When he arrived at his base at Nha Trang, he was immediately informed that a new aviation brigade was being formed at Da Nang and they desperately needed Chinook pilots.

"I jumped on a plane and reported to the brigade commander at Da Nang, and told him I was there to fly Chinooks. The first thing he said to me was 'David I don't know why they assigned you to me. We're overmanned with Chinook pilots.'"

Although he was disappointed, David managed to brush it aside and asked what other jobs were available, obviously hoping for a flying billet.

"'I don't know what to do with you David,' the brigade commander told me. 'But here's something you might be interested in,' he said pulling a paper from his in-box. 'MACV, down in Saigon, wants somebody who is aviation and infantry qualified and knows about Vietnam to do some kind of briefing with the news media. They're taking one major from each of the four corps, to interview for the job. Would you be interested in something like that?'

"I would sure like to know more about it," I answered. "So I hitched a ride on the next plane and flew to Saigon. There were three other majors at MACV Headquarters interviewing for what turned out to be a MACV briefer for the Five O'clock Follies, although it wasn't called that at the time. The briefings were actually held at 1645 (4:45 p.m.). I liked what I heard so I called Da Nang and told the brigade commander that I wasn't coming back."

Each day David would type up a morning press release for that day's brief. "Our source of information was the command information center, which was highly classified. The information came in from the field. We would take whatever looked interesting from that information to highlight the previous day's activities. That was the basis for the morning communiqué. We would continually update our information throughout the day, so when it was time for the follies we had a pretty good idea of what was going on in South Vietnam on that particular day," David said.

David said that the briefing officers would sometimes run into problems because anytime U.S. and South Vietnamese units were on joint operations, each side would give separate reports, which generally presented totally different views. These conflicting reports forced David and the other MACV briefing officers to agree to a compromise.

"If, for example, the South Vietnamese said 160 Viet Cong had been killed, and the American report said that only 60 of the enemy were killed, we would compromise and say 75 Viet Cong had been killed. That's how we got into the whole body count thing," David said. Compromises such, as that was the major reason, according to David, for the news media's distrust of the daily briefings.

"Every journalist in Saigon went to the "Five O' Clock Follies, just to hear the latest propaganda," a veteran Associated Press correspondent told a gathering of newspaper editors in 1985. "Afterwards we'd go to the Continental Palace, just a couple of blocks away, for a drink. The Continental's terrace was a terrific news exchange. We'd sit there and hash over what we had just heard. Invariably somebody who had just had an interview with (General William) Westmoreland, or some other high-ranking officer, would say, 'but that's not what Westy (or whoever) had to say about this or that operation.' So we'd sort of fit that together with whatever was said at the follies and file our stories."

MACV's compromised briefs also led to a less than flattering creation of *The Battle Hymn of the Vietnam Journalist*, which Western journalists would belt out to the tune of "Battle Hymn of the Republic" after a few drinks on the Continental Palace terrace.

Mine eyes have seen the story of the winning of the war.
It is published every afternoon, a little past four.
They put it in the briefing sheet, and they tell us no more.
And the truth goes sliding by.
Glory, glory oh MACV communiqué,
Glory, glory for the things it has to say.
Glory, glory how it brightens our day,
And the truth goes sliding by.
Three hundred-fifty sorties, but there is no BDA.

A reporter then asks a question, and that completes the day,
And the truth goes sliding by.
The Pentagon worked out a plan; it wasn't just a stunt.
But due to a lack of choppers, there was just a single grunt.
So they put him up at Con Thien, and made themselves a front.
And the truth goes sliding by.

But despite the mistrust, David said he and his fellow briefers always tried to put out true and accurate information. "The problem," David said, "was the simple fact that there were more than 500 accredited news media representatives in county at any given time. These people had the ability to hop on a C-130 in the morning, fly to Da Nang for a Marine operation and watch 15 body bags being loaded onto a helicopter after the operation was over. They would then fly back to Saigon in time for the briefings.

"The best information we had would say five Marines had been killed. Of course as soon as we would say that, a hand would shoot up and the reporter would say 'I was on that operation and I saw them carry out 15 body bags. Why you're lying to us, major?'

"Our response would be, 'well this is the latest report we have.' Later I would go back and check it out, and unfortunately the reporter would more often than not be right. In the haste to provide us with information, so we could brief the media, mistakes were made," David said, "but we never knowingly tried to deceive the media, no matter what the situation. We did make a number of blunders," David admits, "but there was never any attempt to deliberately deceive the media and the American public. Eighty-five percent of the news that came out of Vietnam came from the daily press briefings and I would say that 95 percent of the news reported was accurate."

Colonel David retired from active duty in 1983 and settled in the Gulf of Mexico resort community of Orange Beach, Alabama.

###

Charles Butts:

Cholera, typhoid, bubonic plague

In May 1953, Charles Butts enlisted in the United States Navy and was off to boot camp in Great Lakes, Illinois. By the time Butts graduated from boot camp the Korean War was winding down, so he settled in for more than a decade as a Navy corpsman.

In 1964 Senior Chief Hospitalman Charles Butts was commissioned as an ensign in the Navy Medical Service Corps. He and four other sailors began school at San Jose State College, San Jose, California, studying environmental health.

Because of a shortage of medical personnel in Vietnam, Butts and two of his classmates were issued orders and arrived in Vietnam December 31, 1967, but the three men were sent to different areas. Butts, now a lieutenant was attached to the Preventive Medicine Section, First Medical Battalion, First Marine Division, based at Da Nang, but was sent northwest to Phu Bai.

Butts traveled to different hamlets via helicopter or jeep, depending upon availability, to search out and correct potential health hazards involving cholera, typhoid, rabies and bubonic plague within the different hamlets.

He had only been in Vietnam a few weeks when the jeep he and his driver, a Marine corporal, were riding in hit a land mine. Butts explained that the two of them were protected from the worst of the blast by sandbags tied to the jeep, but he was thrown from the vehicle and landed in a rice paddy 50 feet from the jeep. Laughing, he said, "I was thankful for that rice paddy. It made for a soft landing.

A few months later the twosome were driving between hamlets when the driver noticed a Vietnamese child standing next to a bridge with his hands over his ears. Suspecting there was something wrong, the men decided to inspect the bridge before driving across. They found a satchel bomb attached to the bridge that was set to explode when the jeep drove across.

One of Butts' most memorable events occurred when a Navy corpsman became suspicious after most of the villagers in the village of Lan Co, in Thua Thien Province, developed a sickness. The corpsman's instincts were correct; the problem was bubonic plague. Despite the risk of infection to himself and his team, Butts, accompanied by an entomologist, volunteered to take a hypodermic jet injector apparatus crew, and go to the village to immunize the population against bubonic plague. To make the situation worse, the jet apparatus for the hypodermic malfunctioned. Through an interpreter, Butts was able to keep the people at the dispensary while the instrument was repaired and then he and his team of three corpsmen inoculated 3,300 Vietnamese over a two-day period.

"That was quite an experience," Butts recalls. "Early in the morning we would inoculate very young children and elderly people. Then, about 10 o'clock we would get this influx of young men that we were pretty positive were Viet Cong, but still we took care of them. They didn't harm us at the time because they knew we were helping them. We felt we were pretty safe in the village during the daylight hours because we were helping people. But at night we would leave and come back after sunrise."

Butts explained that when the sun began to set, the team would get a little nervous, but just as it was getting dark a Marine helicopter always picked them up. We were never so glad to see anybody in our lives" Butts said.

"One of the biggest problems we had in Vietnam," says Butts, "was just staying alive because there was no safe place over there."

Referring to another incident Butts said, "We were scheduled to go to another military outpost to search for health hazards, but for some reason we couldn't get transportation. The next morning we learned that the entire outpost had been wiped out by a massive land attack; everyone in the area was killed," butts, said remorsefully.

A number of the Marines were found on their knees with their hands tied behind their back, shot in the back of the head execution style. It was the type of warfare you can never be trained for. You can try to explain to people what it was like, but unless they were there they can never understand what it was really like. What makes the whole Vietnam experience even worse," says Butts, "is the fact that Vietnam veterans came home to people throwing rotten tomatoes and lettuce at them and calling them 'baby killers.' It took me a long time to get over my resentment of politicians and the American government in general," he said.

Butts retired from the Navy as a lieutenant commander in October 1977.

###

Doc Kunkle:
Friends stick together

One mid-summer day in 1966, a fresh high school graduate, because of poor job opportunities in the metropolitan area of Pittsburgh, Pennsylvania, walked into a downtown recruiting office to enlist in the Air Force. Not realizing the Air Force and Marine Corps had swapped spaces; Doc Kunkle turned into what had been the Air Force office.

A few days later he found himself in boot camp at Parris Island, South Carolina, the first step of what would turn out to be a 20-year adventure.

"I was actually enrolled at Penn State at the time, but they had no deferment for GPA at the time, and rather than risk getting drafted by the Army, I had decided to enlist so I could choose my branch of service," says Kunkle. "Everyone on my dad's side of the family had been Air Force. But the Marine Corps recruiter started talking about aviation, and I liked his pitch. So I went ahead and enlisted."

After boot camp Kunkle went to aviation structural mechanic school and upon graduation reported to his first duty station at Marine Corps Air Station, Beaufort, South Carolina. In February 1967, when a lot of young men his age were either burning their draft cards or fleeing to Canada, Kunkle decided he wanted to go to Vietnam.

"A lot of my friends were going over. There's this thing called camaraderie in the service," says Kunkle. "And I wanted to make my contribution in the military with my friends, so I also volunteered."

Kunkle recalls that in a matter of weeks he was in combat training at Camp Pendleton, California, and hardly before he knew it, he was aboard a C-130 headed for Chu Lai, South Vietnam. Chu Lai, according to Kunkle, was manned by a composite of the military services.

"We had Navy Seabees who did road and runway construction, Army personnel who maintained the safety of the perimeter, and several Marine Corps aviation commands."

Kunkle recalls that his first three days at his new duty station could have made a great situation for a "M.A.S.H."—type TV show.

"After we unloaded from the C-130, we were put in these (troop transport) trucks and dropped off at our plywood huts. When I walked into my hut, there were cots and stuff inside, but I was the only person. I had my C-rations my weapon, my helmet, and I thought that was my spot in Vietnam. I sat in a corner of the hut with my rifle on one side and my C-rations on the other for three days and three nights. I didn't go out because I thought the Viet Cong (VC) were just over the next sand dune waiting to kill me. I stayed right there—didn't shave or bathe the whole time."

Kunkle later learned that he was the first of his group to arrive; his colleagues had not yet arrived from Japan. "Finally, one of my co-workers came in and asked why I hadn't been showing up for work. So I told him."

Once Kunkle saw the light of day outside his hut, he quickly got in step with the rest of his unit. But his concerns about the VC being just beyond the next sand dune were not far from fact.

"Infiltrators would come in and put satchel bombs in the exhausts of the Skyhawks on the airstrip," he says. When the plane was started it would explode. Another major concern was incoming mortar and missile fire from a nearby mountain range. We never knew when the VC was going to fire on us. We had sandbag bunkers set up near our huts and near the flight line," he says.

Kunkle, like most American servicemen in Vietnam, had several collateral duties, such as mess duty and guard duty. But his main job, he says, was fixing bullet holes in jet aircraft. "It was our job to keep 'em flying." That wasn't always easy. Kunkle recalls the worst case he encountered. "This one pilot had run out of bullets, and he was chasing down several VC in his jet. This one VC ran into a hut. I guess he thought that he'd be safe in there—bad decision. The pilot flew his jet through the grass hut. He got the VC, but in a manner of speaking the VC also got the plane. The engine was full of FOD (foreign object damage), the wings were all ripped up and the flight control systems were broken," said Kunkle.

Kunkle said that, thanks in large part to the nearby aircraft graveyard from which they were able to cannibalize from non-airworthy aircraft, the plane was flying again in just 30 days.

Broken planes and combat aren't the only things the retired master sergeant recalls about Vietnam. He particularly recalls the morning he woke up in his plywood hut to discover a rat the size of a small dog sitting on his chest. Then there were the coral snakes that would hang over the metal rafters to escape the heat while the troops were showering.

There are also the very unpleasant memories of twice being wounded and wondering if his time had come. In one incident, Kunkle was grazed above his left eyebrow by a sniper's bullet as he walked out of his hut. Another time he and several other Marines were working on the flight line one evening when they encountered VC trying to sneak into the compound. Kunkle was stabbed in the side during hand-to-hand combat while fighting off the infiltrators. It was this kind of daily life and death situation Kunkle says he'll always remember.

"I've never before or since experienced such camaraderie," he says. "You rely on the guy next to you every day for your life. The friendships you develop in that kind of situation are truly unique. You may never see that person again, but they'll always be in your heart and on your mind."

Upon reaching the end of his tour in Vietnam, Kunkle, along with the other men in his unit, volunteered for "one more year" at Chu Lai. "We'd been together since Pendleton," says Kunkle. "I guess we just didn't want to break the gang up."

When Kunkle did finally return stateside in March 1969, he went right back to his old squadron and his old job at Beaufort.

Kunkle, a Batman memorabilia collector and avid tennis player, loves movies. But you'll never find him watching a war movie. "They bring back a lot of old memories—memories that are sometimes too painful to relive."

Kunkle says that at the time, he felt good about what the United States was doing in Vietnam. "American presence allowed the South Vietnamese farmers to continue doing their life's work without the fear of being harassed or killed by the VC. "But," he adds in hindsight, it wasn't worth losing all of those American lives for."

###

Harv Shiplett, Paul Dickson:

The Brave Ones Were Shooting The Enemy...The Crazy Ones Were Shooting Film

Vietnam was the most photographically documented war in history. In addition to the hundreds of accredited news media photographers serving in Vietnam, military photographers were assigned to every facet of the war, on the ground, in the air and on the sea.

And while their civilian colleagues were pretty much free to go wherever they wanted in their pursuit to cover the war, military lensmen frequently still had the upper hand. They were insiders, brothers, members of the family. They wore the same uniforms, ate the same food, slept in the same tents, took the same risks and suffered the same casualties as their fellow warriors.

Although the military photographer had the advantage of being an "insider," in one way the uniform was a drawback. Technically, all the pictures shot by military photographers belonged to the U.S. Government. While the photographer was virtually unrestricted in what he could photograph, many of his pictures, particularly those deemed unsuitable for public viewing, were mysteriously "lost" during the bureaucratic editing process. Photography would be sent, with captions, to an office in the Pentagon for review and release. Since pictures were to be released to the public, releasing authorities were vigilantly alert for classified material or pictures that might put the military in a less-than-flattering light.

In addition to shipboard photographers covering the war from Yankee Station, the Navy also deployed an elite photo operation, known as the Pacific Fleet Combat Camera Group (CCGPAC), which rotated motion picture and still photographers into Vietnam for 120-day tours twice a year. CCGPAC had about 20 photographers in Vietnam at all times during the war. Another elite but smaller group of Navy photographers were assigned to Commander Naval Forces, Vietnam (ComNavForV) and worked directly for the ComNavForV Public Affairs Office.

The work of these Navy photo teams took them from the DMZ (Demilitarized Zone) in the north to the Mekong River Delta in the south. They rode in helicopters, visited forward fire bases, accompanied reconnaissance patrols into the jungle, rode with the crews of Navy PBRs (Patrol Boats, River) and went on fire support missions. The CCG and ComNavForV photographers documented every aspect of the Navy's role in the Vietnam War.

Two of those Navy Vietnam combat shutter clickers are Paul Dickson and Harv Shiplett. Dickson was assigned to CCGPAC while Shiplett served with ComNavForV.

"The first teams of the Pacific Fleet Mobile Photographic Group sent to Vietnam worked out of the unit's Detachment Alfa, in Yokosuka, Japan," said Dickson. "From Yokosuka, the teams were dispatched to Vietnam for specific assignments and returned to Japan when the assignment was complete."

As the war began to heat up, CCGPAC realized that it couldn't adequately perform its mission from Japan, so arrangements were made for a detachment to share space with Seventh Fleet's Detachment Charlie, a public affairs detachment based at the Rex Hotel in downtown Saigon.

"This worked fine for about a year, "Dickson said, "But the distance between the airport and the Rex Hotel and the number of camera teams rotating in and out soon made it necessary for CCG to seek more convenient spaces.

"Besides," Dickson continues, "there was no berthing or messing for anyone coming to Saigon for temporary duty. Upon arriving in Saigon, you had to go from Tan Son Nhut Air Base (the normal arrival point into Saigon) to an office in a downtown hotel to check in and have your orders endorsed. The only place the crews could stay was in a civilian hotel—if they could find one. Hotel rooms in Saigon were scarce and expensive."

To solve the problem CCGPAC rented a villa and obtained several bunk beds and set up a "motel" near Tan Son Nhut for the use of the teams.

"We hired a Vietnamese family to handle the domestic chores, including laundry service," Dickson said. "Meals were 'cook and serve your own.' Rent was charged on a man/day basis. Since we never knew how many people would spend how many days in the villa, the charges were based on the last month's man/day count. The Combat Camera Group Villa quickly became the home-away-from-home for a collection of wandering Seabees, an occasional Marine, fleet public affairs and medical personnel transiting through Saigon.

"Anyone without a place to stay was welcome to fit in wherever they could in the double-decker bunks in the villa."

While Dickson and his combat camera teams were rotating in and out of country every four months or so, Shiplett and his nine-man photo crew in the ComNavForV Public Affairs Office photo lab in Saigon played a more permanent role.

"When I landed in Saigon, it was a real cultural shock," said Shiplett. "It was my first time in Asia. The language, the customs; everything was so different from anything I had experienced. It took some getting used to. During the day the streets of Saigon would be filled with people. Street vendors with push carts, pedicabs, young women in high silk dresses, old men with long, gray beards, American and RVN soldiers, and traffic—complete with the worst drivers I've ever seen.

"There was always something to see and do in Saigon" he continued, "shopping, sightseeing with your camera, drinking and lots of pretty girls. And, it was reasonably safe. At times you could almost forget you were in a war zone. But, when those rare moments occurred, the armed men, sandbagged, barbed wired buildings, and curfew quickly brought you back to reality. If they didn't, the frequent VC alerts would."

As much fun as Saigon could be, Shiplett said he and his photographers looked forward to field assignments. The excitement and adventure of going where the action was, according to the retired combat photographer was hard to resist.

"I remember my first field assignment very well," Shiplett said. "Another photographer and I were sent down to a Navy PBR unit operating in the Delta to document the PBR's escorting several barges up river. Three boats made up the escort. I was riding in the second boat. On our way up river, VC rockets bracketed my boat. All the boats immediately opened fire. For a second I couldn't make up my mind what I wanted to shoot with my camera or my rifle. I clicked off a few quick pictures, then picked up my M-16 and returned fire. It was a brief exchange and the rest of the trip was uneventful but I had received my baptism of fire."

Shiplett recalled another occasion on the river boats that left him with vivid memories to this day. "We were heading down river when we came upon a fuel barge which Charlie (Viet Cong) had attacked just before we arrived. As we slowed to come alongside the barge I saw something floating in the water. At first I thought that it might be a water bomb— a favorite VC tactic for trying to sink one of our boats.

"When I saw that no one else was going to leave their battle station to check it out, I eased over the side and cautiously made my way toward the object. Reaching out to touch the floating object, I was horrified to see that it was an American soldier. "I later learned that the dead American was from my hometown, Detroit, and ironically had lived on the same street that I had lived on when I was growing up there. I don't know if that was supposed to be an omen or what," Shiplett said, "but I do know that I'm still bothered by that after all these years," the retired Navy master chief photographer's mate confesses.

Why anyone would want to go to war armed with cameras rather than a weapon is a question that neither Shiplett nor Dickson has an answer for. Perhaps the best answer lies in the slogan of the International Combat Camera Association— "The brave ones were shooting the enemy: The crazy ones were shooting film."

###

Gary Cooper:

Many Have Never Returned

When Gary Cooper left his hometown of Portsmouth, Ohio in 1958, at the age of 17, to join the Marine Corps, he never dreamed that he would soon be referred to as a "Hollywood Marine."

"With a name like Gary Cooper and going through boot camp at San Diego I became an instant target for some good-natured ribbing," said the retired gunnery sergeant.

"I was in boot camp about six weeks," Cooper said, "when I hear this voice bellow out. 'Cooper to the duty hut!' I go running to the duty hut—scared half to death—and there was my drill instructor standing in the middle of the room, his legs spread and his hands hovering near his hips. 'So you're Gary Cooper? Well, I'm John Wayne and it's time to see who's faster.'

"He then told me that during the remainder of my time in boot camp, anytime we met he was going to call me out. And he did. No matter where we met after that, the drill instructor would yell, 'All right Cooper, draw!'"

Cooper's name and that sort of good-natured ribbing quickly earned him the title of "Hollywood Marine." But there was nothing Hollywood about his 20-year Marine Corps career, particularly his tour in Vietnam.

"The way we went to Vietnam was part of the stress factor associated with that war," said Cooper. "We were rotated in and out as individuals, not as units. I arrived in country as a 24-year-old staff sergeant and I have a bunch of 18-19-year-old Marines looking to me for guidance. As far as they were concerned I was the professional, despite the fact that many of them had been in combat for several months, and I had no actual combat experience whatsoever. That will put a lot of unnecessary stress on anyone. Stress which could have been prevented, had we rotated in and out of country as a unit."

Cooper may not have had any combat experience when he left California for Vietnam, but that experience was quickly acquired, beginning with his arrival at Da Nang in July 1968.

"I flew into Da Nang aboard a C-130 smack into an enemy attack. Charlie was shelling the air strip as we came in for a landing," Cooper recalls. "We taxied all over the place before we finally came to a stop and everyone was rushed off the aircraft and into a shelter."

Although Cooper's background was infantry, he was assigned to the 3rd Battalion, 4th Marines as battalion supply chief, a job, which he quickly discovered, wasn't needed. To make himself more useful, Cooper volunteered to take charge of a 25-30 man defensive unit in an area called "Mississippi."

"After a couple of nights on the line, I decided we really needed some assistance. Our guys were in foxholes, which were only 3- or 4-feet deep. We needed more security than that. I made contact with a Seabee, a second class petty officer, and told him what my problem was. He came back the next day with a bulldozer and a crew. The Seabees dug us some real man-sized, sandbagged, fighting holes.

"I developed a lifelong respect for the Seabees as a result of that little operation," the gunny said with admiration in his voice. "One of the Seabees was wounded while operating the bulldozer and when the corpsman and I got to him we saw that he was wearing only a T-shirt. 'Man if you had been wearing your flak jacket you wouldn't have gotten hurt,' I told him. 'I don't like those things, gunny,' he told me, 'they're too hot. Besides, now I get to go home.'"

Other events involving the Viet Cong didn't end as well. In one case, Cooper recalls a little one-legged orphan boy who was killed by the Viet Cong because he tipped off the Americans about a minefield.

"I was attached to the 12th Marines at the time,' Cooper said, "and I was assigned to a mine-sweeping detail. Two other staff NCOs and myself took turns sweeping an area near a bridge, which Charlie repeatedly mined. We would clear them out during the day and Charlie would replant them at night. Anyway, this boy, we called him Little Charlie, hung around the area all night, and when we arrived in the morning for our daily sweep, Little Charlie would tell us where he thought Charlie had placed new mines. Ninety percent of the time he was right. No telling how many lives Little Charlie saved by informing us where the Viet Cong had placed mines.

"This went on for several months then Little Charlie quit showing up. I later found out that the Viet Cong had caught him. I can only assume that he was killed.

"This sort of thing just added to the stress factor that we all had to endure. I can still remember when I was at Da Nang. We would come in from the bush to air conditioned quarters, nice NCO and officers' clubs and USO shows. Now don't get me wrong, those were nice things, but they also sort of left the impression that the war wasn't something that we needed to take too seriously.

"We were well aware of the anti-war protests taking place back home. But what we didn't know about were the things we weren't being told by the politicians and our own military leaders. And of course when we did get home we were treated like criminals. Why? Because we did what our government—which we believed in with all our heart—asked us to do."

After returning home from Vietnam in July 1969, Gunnery Sgt. Cooper, like many of his fellow Vietnam vets, suffered through years of anguish trying to come to grips with the experience of Vietnam. And like numerous other Vietnam veterans, Cooper says he has forgiven what he and many Vietnam vets consider a betrayal by the nation. "For many Vietnam vets," says Cooper, "the shooting ended years ago. But in their hearts, many of them are still waiting to come home."

"I can forgive, but I can't forget," he said. "I'll always think of Vietnam as a period of waiting. Waiting to go. Waiting to fight. Waiting to die. Waiting to go home. Waiting to be welcomed home.

The first four we've achieved. The fifth we're still waiting for.

###

Norman Higgins:

Cemetery Siege

Major Norman Higgins was a wing safety officer with the 31st Tactical Fighter Wing, Homestead Air Force Base, Homestead, Florida, when he received orders for Vietnam in January 1969. "We were flying F-100Cs and I flew about six missions a week," Higgins said.

Several months later, Higgins and his wingman were flying a rather routine mission over Vietnam when they were rerouted in flight. Their new mission would help save the lives of several soldiers, one of whom Higgins would "accidentally" meet years later.

"It was sometime in the fall time frame and we were headed up north to Laos," Higgins recalled, when we were diverted. When my wingman, Reed Richards, and I reached our new target there was a flight of A-4s already making bombing runs from North to South. Our mission was to bomb a cemetery.

The cemetery was surrounded by a concrete wall with an archway built into the east wall. NVA (North Vietnam regulars) soldiers were heavily entrenched in the cemetery. We later found out that the NVA had built a network of tunnels and bunkers underneath the cemetery.

Because of the monsoon season the pilots were facing low cloud cover, so they had to fly out to sea, turn around and fly back along the Bong Is River underneath a 3,500-foot ceiling. "That meant flying 500 feet below the ceiling because Army helicopters would fly next to the ceiling," Higgins explains.

"We got in touch with the Forward Air Controller (FAC) and he told us the First Air Calvary and Second ARVN (Army of the Republic of Vietnam) had been tied up in a heavy battle with the NVA for quite some time. I made a pass then Reed made a pass then the FAC told us to 'hold high.' I asked him what the problem was and he said 'every time you roll in small arms automatic weapons systems are firing at you.' I asked if it was small arms fire (rifle) and the FAC said 'no, 14mm, which is comparable to our 50-caliber machine gun."

When Higgins rolled in for his next pass he saw where the fire was coming from. "There was a hootch down there with a ditch all the way around it and I could see the flashes.

"When you see automatic fire coming at you it looks like red roses blossoming; they look real red."

Higgins rolled off and told the FAC he knew where the fire was coming from and told the FAC he could hit the target. "I told Reed where it was and told him we would drop napalm in there. We each dropped two 750 pounders. We made one pass each so we could drop them one at a time, and stack them on each other. We filled that ditch, all the way up to the mountain base with napalm and the firing stopped."

"We could see NVA running and we strafed them. After that we were Winchester (out of ordinance), so we were given a RTB (return to base). As we were about to leave the FAC told us that the ground commander wanted to speak with us. OK, I answered and the ground commander came on the air. 'I want to thank y'all because now we can resupply and get our dead and wounded out. We have been unable to do that for seven days.' Reed and I wiggled our wings in a salute and returned to base."

At that time Higgins couldn't know that 29 years later he would meet one of the troops he helped save, Edward Krumwiede, at a Bible College in Pensacola, Florida.

As the two planes prepared to RTB, the pilots preformed an off-target battle damage assessment, a process in which each pilot does a visual inspection of his partner's plane to ensure no fluids are leaking from their plane.

"Reed pulled away from me and I asked him what was wrong?"

"You have a hole in your canopy, right behind your head," Richards said.

Higgins hadn't noticed when it happened, but after checking Richard's plane the two returned to base and upon landing taxied to the de-arming area. "I looked back and saw the hole about the size of a lemon in my canopy.

"What had happened was a 50-caliber shell had come in and had impacted in the headrest of my seat. The headrest is made out of steel, so that if you have to eject it will knock right through the canopy, so that's the only thing that saved me.

For ending the cemetery siege, both Higgins and Richards were awarded the Distinguished Flying Cross for valor. "I never asked for that or any decoration over there," Higgins said. "The only decoration I wanted was red, green and yellow (the Vietnam Service Medal). That's the one that said I had been there. I went over there to do a job and I did that job," Higgins said. "I have no regrets. I probably would have fought the war differently, but I was a regular Air Force officer, so whether or not I agreed with the political aspects made no difference."

"You know you see atrocities of war and you sometimes get wrapped up in the war. You go out every day and drop bombs on people, even though you don't always see them it begins to wear on you after a while. One of the most humane missions I had was when we were called in to hit a village that had been taken over by the NVA.

"It was a large village on the beach surrounded by rice paddies. Someone was firing at me from a hootch inside the village. The hootch had a rice straw roof, so I strafed the hootch with 20mm cannon and the roof began to burn. Someone ran out of the hooch and started running along the dike between the rice paddies.

"Something told me, 'don't fire, don't fire! I told FAC I was rolling off dry. I looked back over the wing, and I'm only about 60 feet off the ground. There was a woman running. At first I thought she had a bundle of clothes until I got close enough to see that it was a baby. So, I pulled off and told my wingman not to strafe the person on the ground because it was a woman with a baby. She turned and went north across the dike and got out of the village."

###

Edward R. Krumwiede:

Call for Napalm

Unlike most American troops in Vietnam who spent the majority of their in-country tour in one, maybe two locations, Edward R. Krumwiede's first 30 days in country were reminiscent of a travel agency-arranged tour.

"I entered the country at Saigon in August 1968 and within 30 days had been sent to a total of four different bases, ranging from Saigon to Da Nang," said the former Army Specialist Five (Spc.5).

After his "tour" of Vietnam, the then 23-year-old soldier finally settled down at Long Bian.

Although Krumwiede was assigned to the Army engineers, he says he actually worked wherever he was needed. Like many Vietnam veterans, Krumwiede says that although he can't recall every detail of his year-long tour in Vietnam, he does recall landing in Vietnam and his first few days in country. "We came into Saigon aboard a TWA flight about 11:30 a.m.," said Krumwiede. "Man, when they opened those doors. Wow! It was like stepping into an oven. Besides that, it was lunch time so I was assigned KP."

A couple of days later, Krumwiede and nearly 90 other soldiers boarded a C-130 at Tan Son Nhut Air Base and flew to Da Nang. "The first night we were in Da Nang," Krumwiede said, "we got hit. Wow! They really zapped us. I was awakened around midnight and all I could see was rockets—whoosh, whoosh, whoosh, whoosh! The night was lit up like day. Those things seemed to be coming from everywhere.

"As I recall the Marines took a number of causalities, but fortunately I came through it OK.

After three or four days at Da Nang, I boarded another C-130 for Quang Tri where I finally joined my outfit—the 1st LOG, 71st Battalion.

"Wow! Quang Tri was the wilderness. But what made it even worse, no one had ever heard of my outfit. That didn't mean I was going back to Da Nang or Saigon, however. I was put in a transportation company. It wasn't long after that, before they located my company and I was reassigned. When I finally hooked up with my outfit I was in for another rude awakening. The place was dirty, there was no chow hall, and we ate out in the open—like a big cook out every day. Some of the guys said they hadn't had a shower for weeks... I certainly had no reason to disbelieve them," Krumwiede laughed. "It certainly wasn't much of a duty station."

"At times we would get attack alerts, but not much would happen. Then one night, shortly before Tet of '69 we got hit really hard. An estimated 200 VC attacked. They swarmed over the wire and blew up everything they could. One charge went off about five feet from my hootch. That one really got my attention," Krumwiede, says with a smile.

"That night, just before attacking us, Charlie launched a rocket attack on a transportation unit just a short distance from us. I believe five or six guys got it there, but my unit managed to escape without any personnel casualties. They did a lot of damage to our trucks and destroyed the general's quarters, but other than that my company came through it all right.

"Of the 200 or so VC that hit us, only about two or three actually got into the compound and they were killed immediately. The others retreated to a cemetery not far from our compound. They had at least a regiment under there. Well the Air Force was called in for a napalm strike on the cemetery. By now its daylight and we could see the planes come in and drop their napalm. Needless to say that eliminated any VC activity in that area."

Though he had no way of knowing it at the time, Krumwiede and the pilot of the first plane to drop a load of napalm on the VC stronghold, Major Norman Higgins, would meet again 29 years later at a Bible college in the Florida Panhandle.

"I remember talking with a fellow Vietnam vet at Pensacola Bible College about the cemetery incident," Krumwiede said, "and he mentioned something about dropping napalm on a cemetery. So we start comparing notes and lo-and-behold, it turns out that he was the Air Force pilot who made the first napalm strike on the cemetery stronghold at Long Bian. Norm was a fighter pilot and I later found out that the North Vietnamese had placed a bounty on him."

In looking back on his tour in Vietnam, Krumwiede, who has made several trips back to Vietnam, says he found the Vietnamese people to be hard working individuals who are trying desperately to rebuild their country. "I went back to Vietnam for the first time in 1998, Krumwiede said, because there were still a lot of things that bothered me. Going back really helped me, as it has many other veterans. I guess the hardest thing about going back was actually touching down in Saigon.

"That brought back a lot of bad memories. But I must say the people couldn't have been nicer. It was a very pleasant experience. An experience that I would recommend for every Vietnam veteran seeking final closure."

###

Terry Sanders:

<u>Have Tool Belt Will Travel</u>

Except for the constant threat of attack, duty in Vietnam for 20-year-old Terry Sanders of Bedford, Indiana, wasn't all that much different than working on a construction site in the United States. His duties took him from one construction site to another ranging from Da Nang to Cam Ranh Bay.

Sanders, a member of the Navy Seabees, the Navy's elite construction force, recalled his arrival at Da Nang in April 1969 with less than fond memories.

"My very first assignment in country, was standing shore patrol at Da Nang. Me and another guy, who had arrived at Da Nang with me from Travis Air Force Base, California, were assigned to patrol a six-block barracks and club area. Standing shore patrol," Sanders grimaced, "was something I thought I had left behind in the states."

Standing shore patrol wasn't the only thing Sanders disliked about Da Nang, however. After two days at the sprawling air base, Sanders, along with a dozen or so other new arrivals attended an "in country" briefing where a request was made for Seabee volunteers for one of several in country mobile construction teams which traveled throughout South Vietnam.

"I think my hand was probably one of the first to shoot up," the former Seabee said. "After the night I had just had I wanted out of Da Nang as quickly as possible."

The night in question—Sanders' second night in Vietnam—Da Nang came under a rocket and mortar attack.

"I was trying to find out where the weapons were and where my defensive position was, and I was told to get my butt in a bunker and sit it out. That certainly didn't make me feel any more comfortable, so when they asked for volunteers I was ready to go."

The following day he left Da Nang for Chu Lai. At Chu Lai he was at last issued weapons and given further briefings before being as-

164

signed to a six-man construction team and dispatched to Quang Ngai, a mountainous region south of Chu Lai.

The team's first assignment was to construct an advance base for a South Vietnamese Ranger unit in the mountains west of Quang Ngai.

"What should have been a fairly simple job took more than seven weeks," Sanders recalls. "Every time we would get the base nearly finished, Charlie would walk mortars in and blow it up. It was getting a bit scary.

"My birthday is June 2," Sanders said. "About 2 a.m., June 2, 1969, we were back in the compound at Quang Ngai, when we got hit real bad. I was actually wondering if I was going to still be around at sunrise to see my 21st birthday," the former Seabee said, his eyes still revealing the fear after more than 30 years.

"Luckily I did make it. But we did take some casualties. The base itself, however, received only minor damage but three of the bridges coming into the town had been blown up. Daylight also revealed that Charlie had paid a high price for his unsuccessful attack. There was 40 or 50 dead VC in the wire," Sanders said.

After the June 2 attack, the Seabee team at Quang Ngai was split up and Sanders was reassigned to MACV Team 16 at a joint operations base known as Camp Pane.

In his new assignment, Petty Officer Sanders was placed in charge of two South Vietnamese nationals and assigned the responsibility for providing routine maintenance and keeping electrical power supplied to the base.

"We didn't have too awful many of the niceties at Camp Pane that we take for granted, such as urinals and showers," Sanders remembers.

"I managed to get a few urinals from Chu Lai and we hooked up several 55-gallon drums and made water towers out of them for showers. These little things made life a whole lot nicer for all of us. Actually," Sanders says with pride, "we had the only urinals south of Chu Lai."

Life at Camp Pane was far from a day at the beach, however. One horrible incident in particular Sanders remembers all too well. "There was some real heavy contact between American troops and the NVA just to the north of us. I recall an APC (armored personnel carrier) which had taken an RPG (rocket propelled grenade) right on one of the corners, one of the weakest points on the vehicle; went inside and bounced around before exploding. When we dropped the ramp, blood, bones and human parts came flowing out. Only two of the 18 guys inside survived. These are the terrible sort of things you would like to forget, but can't," Sanders said.

It was a short time later, Sanders recalls, when the Naval Support Activity at Da Nang "discovered" where he was at and decided to pull him out of the MACV team. According to Sanders, the Army major in charge of the camp put up a fight to keep him at Camp Pane but he was only able to delay Sanders' reassignment for a short time.

Within a matter of days after that, Sanders, an electrician, found himself hundreds of miles south at Cam Ranh Bay.

"I was assigned to CBMU-302. I stayed in the big city of Cam Ranh Bay for two whole days," he smiled, "and went out with a 10-man team, to build a base for the South Vietnamese Navy. We took our equipment; dump trucks, cement mixer, and a few other vehicles, to Nha Trang and set up a base camp with the White Horse Division—a South Korean Marine Division."

Building of the base, according to the Seabee, meant starting from ground zero.

"The base we were building was actually on a small island. To get to the base, the first thing we had to do was build a floating bridge to the island. Once that was done, we graded the ground, poured concrete— which we had to load by hand—build block houses for the families of the Vietnamese sailors, put in a sewage system, string electrical lines, whatever it took to build a base, that's what we did."

Petty Officer Sanders spent the remainder of his tour in Vietnam with CBMU-302. He returned to the states in 1970 and returned to his hometown of Bedford.

Sanders says that in looking back on the Vietnam War, he strongly feels that the United States was right in being there, but he is strongly opposed to the way the war was waged.

"You can't go in with limited rules of engagement against a foe that doesn't follow those rules," Sanders said thoughtfully. "If we're going to go to war we must be determined to win it and let our military leaders make the decisions, like we did in Desert Storm."

###

David Seiler:
<u>**A Matter of Choice**</u>

David Seiler was about to enter his senior year in college. He was captain of the wrestling team and had a deferment from the Korean War. But, on July 13, 1951, Seiler dropped out of school and enlisted in the Marine Corps and went to Korea.

"I didn't believe in the law that deferred college students. My brother and I joined the Marine Corps together," Seiler said.

In 1953 David Seiler was commissioned and in 1961, under the "Bootstrap" program, took a one-year leave of absence from the Marine Corps, finished college and returned to the service.

In June 1969, Lieutenant Colonel Col. David Seiler, then 40, arrived in Vietnam, as battalion commander of 3rd Battalion, 3rd Regiment, 3rd Marine Division, which was positioned near the Demilitarized Zone (DMZ).

"It (the war), of course was a very big occasion in everybody's life. In spite of the fact that we had so many people over there, it was a different experience for each one," Seiler said.

Less than a month after Seiler's arrival in Vietnam, his command was reassigned to Okinawa. Seiler laughed and called it a "flag and Bible" transfer, meaning nothing was left behind—except their commanding officer. Seiler requested to stay in Vietnam and at that time it was a request the government gladly accepted.

"By staying in Vietnam I had the fortunate experience of becoming the commanding officer of a Combined Action Group (CAG). It was the only pacification program that really worked," Seiler said.

Seiler's command included four companies of Marines, each company made up of 12 to 29 Combined Action Platoons (CAP), each platoon contained four squads of 13 Marines and a Navy corpsman.

According to Seiler, CAG's job was to work on a program that no one thought would work; the Marines were to work with the Popular

Forces (PF), the lowest level of the Vietnamese military. Each squad was teamed up with a squad of PFs.

The Popular Forces were Vietnamese soldiers who worked regular jobs during the day and went out on patrols and ambushes with the Marines at night. There was no designated leader, but Seiler said that at the beginning, a Marine corporal or sergeant would tend to fill the unofficial position of leader.

"What made this whole thing unique and why it worked was that no one was in charge; the Marines were not in charge of the Vietnamese, the Vietnamese were not in charge of the Marines. It was a shared responsibility. However, the strongest person took charge."

"Toward the end of my tour I had come to realize the Vietnamese sergeants were taking over the action of the units. They had gained enough confidence that the Vietnamese sergeant would select where they would go on patrol.

"We gave them the backbone and they provided the intelligence, planning and action," Seiler said. "In effect the Vietnamese took over, and our job was finished."

With pride for his men in his voice, Seiler said. "What made these units work were the young Marines, either a corporal or a sergeant, in charge out in a village away from anywhere else, and what we told them was, 'if you get in trouble, don't worry, we'll be there at first light, but in the meantime, you're all on your own.'

"A number of people told us, 'the Marines are good, but you're expecting too much of a 20-or 21-year-old Marine... that the whole program is doomed to failure,' but we had Marines that made it work. They found out what had to be done and they did it."

Although the corporal or sergeant was in control, Seiler explained that at night he would sometimes rotate among these different squads and go on patrol with them.

"The Vietnamese had a vested interest; they were defending their hamlet or their group of hamlets. They knew who the Viet

Cong were and they knew the area. They (the Popular Forces) would not allow us to go into a place we shouldn't go into, as opposed to some of our regular units who would go wherever they wanted to. They kept us out of trouble; they were our intelligence forces.

"The biggest problem we had was getting the Vietnamese to fight. The Marines wanted to fight all the time and it took a while for us to learn, 'hey, we better listen to these people.'"

Seiler's Marines were in what he called "an Army area. There were no Marine units in the area so, the Army (1st Cavalry Division, My Lai) took care of us," Seiler said.

The Army used the Combined Unit Program (CUP). The Soldiers were in platoon-size units with a lieutenant in command, making the Army units large enough to defend themselves.

Seiler explained that because of their size, the Army units felt they didn't need any help from the Vietnamese.

Comparing the size of the Marine squads to the Army platoons, Seiler said, "We were too small, we needed the Vietnamese. I had about 500 Marines in 50 hamlets who accounted for more daily enemy casualties than an entire Army division."

"The Army did right by us, though," Seiler said. "If a gunny (gunnery sergeant) asked for something such as artillery support or medical help, it was given to us with the same speed as if it had been requested by a lieutenant colonel. The Marine units were respected by the Army."

Laughing, Seiler referred to an incident that took place one night while he was on patrol with one of his squads. He said two Vietnamese soldiers approached him and began to touch him and rub his hands.

Not knowing who these men were he immediately became upset and demanded to know who they were and what they were doing. To Seiler's surprise, the Vietnamese soldiers were assigned to him as bodyguards. By rubbing and touching him they believed that no bullets would pass through him unless they had gone through them first.

As proud as Seiler was of his Marines, he was even more proud of the Navy corpsmen assigned to the Marine squads. "These guys would perform amputations, deliver babies, and hold regular sick call for the villagers as the Marines moved from hamlet to hamlet. The corpsman would set up his medical station and the villagers would come to him to get what would probably be the only medical help they could get. The corpsmen were given the authority to call in military helicopter support to carry civilians to hospitals. Those guys are all heroes in my opinion. The medical help they provided played a large part in gaining the support of the Vietnamese. It was more than providing security, we were looking after them," Seiler said

One of the Marines under Seiler's command, Lance Corporal Miguel Keith, received the Medal of Honor in 1970. "I spoken with Keith one morning and that evening he was killed while saving the lives of the other Marines in his squad."

According to the Medal of Honor citation, Keith was a machine gunner assigned to Combined Action Platoon 132 in Quang Ngai. Keith was wounded while the unit was under attack by enemy forces. He exposed himself to check the security of vital defense positions. He eliminated three enemy soldiers, but was knocked to the ground by an exploding grenade. Keith stood up and began to fire on approximately 25 enemy soldiers who were preparing for a mass attack. Keith eliminated four of the 25 and forced the remaining 21 enemy soldiers to flee.

Seiler rotated out of Vietnam in June 1970, but 29 years later, August 1999, he returned to Vietnam as part of a 12-day military historic tour.

"We were well received by the Vietnamese people. At no time did we run into any resentment," said Seiler, "But, this wasn't like going to France after we had won World War II. We didn't win the Vietnam war."

"A lot of American's were ruined over there and we had a lot of our guys killed or wounded. But, those that survived and served honorably, they have something that nobody can take away from them. I'm glad I went back. It was closure for a lot of people, especially the ones who had been wounded. It wasn't quite the same for me. I was 40 when I went to Vietnam. I was already a career Marine; it was my job."For me it was very worthwhile to make the return trip to Vietnam. I would recommend it to other Vietnam vets.

###

Larry Draeger:

Beginning, Middle, End; He Saw it All

When Larry Draeger joined the Navy in 1959 he never thought he would be witness to basically the beginning and ending of the decade-long Vietnam War.

He joined the Navy after high school in California when he received a "notice" from the Army. "I didn't open the envelope," he said. "I could see in it, though, and I could see a report date."

Draeger said there was "no way" he was going into the Army. "I took the envelope to a Navy recruiter and said, 'Give this back to the senders.'" With that, Draeger snubbed one "invitation" and accepted another with the Navy.

Only three years into his career, he would not only be there when the first U.S. plane was acknowledged as lost in Vietnam, but he would be back and be part of some of the most dramatic scenes in history at the close of the war.

"From 1962 to '65, I made three deployments to Southeast Asia with VA-112 onboard the USS Kitty Hawk. We were at sea for periods of time up to 120 days without ever pulling into port. It was in late '63 or early '64 that the Kitty Hawk crew learned that the United States was acknowledging its first loss of an U.S. aircraft in Vietnam. But never did any of us think it would last as long as it did," he said. "We simply thought, 'we're going to get this over with and get out of there.'"

After a tour of shore duty Draeger returned to sea aboard the USS Coral Sea (CVA-43) for his fourth deployment to Southeast Asia.

In 1975 he was assigned to the USS Midway (CVA-41). "I was the squadron aircraft maintenance chief in VA-93," he said. Now it had been more than 10 years since his first Vietnam deployment and the Midway was sent to the gun line. It was Draeger's fifth time off the coast of Vietnam. "I thought to myself, 'when is this war ever going to end? Is it going too ever end? Why is it continually dragging out?" But it would end soon.

"We began to realize with the (South Vietnamese) government collapsing, things were beginning to wind down," he said. "When it became evident there would be refugees, we had to take all of our airplanes, anything associated with aircraft off the flight deck and store them down in the hangar bays in anticipation of helicopters coming in filled with refugees." The anticipation didn't last long.

"When the evacuation really began to go the helos would come in— stolen helos or whatever—all used in the war effort, piloted by whomever, usually South Vietnamese on one way trips," he said. "The people would get out and as soon as the rotors stopped, we would push the helos over the side. Just as far as you could see in the sky, there was helo after helo, after helo, coming aboard.

"We had to push them off the side because there was no place to keep them on the ship and they couldn't go back to Vietnam; really one-way trips," he said.

"It seems like it lasted about three days. I was up on deck once watching people get out of the helos and the skipper came on (the intercom) saying 'OK, we're going to clear the flight deck because we have a small airplane we're going to recover."

A South Vietnamese Air Force major had flown over the ship and dropped a note saying he and his family were onboard. "We cleared the flight deck and headed into the wind making it a landing strip. As he came in, he was going into the wind too, cut his engine and just kind of eased down on the flight deck. Everyone went crazy-clapping and shouting in joy."

The major and his family became part of the Midway refugees. There were thousands of refugees onboard Midway as well as on other ships off the Vietnam coast. "Vietnamese were housed everywhere there was a place on board even under airplanes. They were everywhere."

Midway then made its way to the Philippines to off-load the refugees, most of who eventually were relocated to the United States.

One day while visiting the National Museum of Naval Aviation in Pensacola, Florida, Draeger got a shock. "There was the airplane the South Vietnamese major landed on the Midway hanging from the ceiling in the museum," he said. "It was like someone kicked me in the stomach. When I saw it, it was like a flashback for a couple of seconds. I could hear the sounds of the people and noise, the cheering—it was so real."

The plane can still be seen at the museum.

###

DESERT STORM

(WAR WITH IRAQ)

1990–1991

William D. Sullivan:

Into the Eye of the Storm

During the summer of 1990, Rear Admiral William D. Sullivan, then a commander, was riding the crest of a dream. He was preparing to assume command of the guided-missile destroyer USS Sampson (DDG-10) home-ported at Mayport, Florida. The change of command was scheduled for August 3, 1990, and the Sampson was to set to sail for the Mediterranean and a six-month deployment with the USS Saratoga (CV-60) carrier battle group four days later. All that changed on August 2, when Iraq invaded Kuwait.

"On the day of the change of command, only one day after the invasion, we weren't sure what the U.S. response would be, but we figured that our deployment schedule was now up in the air," Sullivan remembers. Amid a great deal of speculation about the possibility of war, the battle group and Sampson sailed on schedule on August 7th.

"Sampson had been assigned to the Naval on Call Force Mediterranean— a group of ships from eight NATO countries which traveled around the Mediterranean conducting exercises," says Sullivan.

"It was a fun deployment because you got to visit a number of great liberty ports while also getting some valuable at-sea training during the exercises. It also had a well-deserved reputation as a little bit of a party cruise because in each port there are receptions and social exchanges between the ships. We had loaded out a good supply of beer and wine so we'd be prepared when it was our turn to host a reception," the admiral recalled.

"While transiting the Atlantic, Saratoga received orders to increase speed and proceed directly to Port Said, Egypt, to transit the Suez Canal and take up station in the northern Red Sea. We began to piece together our mission and gain an appreciation for the operation about to unfold. We learned that we were to be part of Operation Desert Shield, and that Sampson's initial mission was to enforce the U.N. sanctions against Iraq. We were to take up station in the northern Red Sea near the entrance to the Gulf of Aqaba and make sure that no shipping carrying prohibited cargo bound for Iraq got through to the port of Aqaba, Jordan. Jordan wasn't sympathetic to the United States and United Nations response to the Iraqi invasion and because it shares a border with Iraq, could have potentially provided an over-land route for prohibited goods to enter Iraq.

"At the time, the Navy wasn't well rehearsed in maritime intercept operations," remembers Sullivan. "The last time we had actively stopped, boarded and searched merchant shipping, was during Operation Market Time in Vietnam. Also at that time we were not yet fully engaged in the Caribbean drug interdiction mission so we didn't have any real recent experience in board and search operations. So we dusted off the procedures for boarding and salvage operations and began figuring out how to do it.

"One thing I do recall vividly," says the admiral, "we had no shortage of volunteers to be on the boarding teams, even though it was a potentially dangerous job. I took care to select only the most physically fit and imposing members of the crew for this job. I wanted the crews of the ships we boarded to think twice before resisting. At the same time, they had to be smart, have the diplomatic skills to properly deal with a cooperative ship, and make command-level decisions in an emergency. We're fortunate that our Navy is well populated with young officers and enlisted personnel who meet that criteria."

As luck would have it, Sampson conducted the first three Red Sea boarding operations of Operation Desert Shield and was the first warship to detect a ship carrying prohibited cargo.

"As I look back on that first boarding now, I have to chuckle," says Sullivan. "You would have thought we were getting ready to conduct the Normandy invasion. I was up all night either on the bridge or in CIC (combat information center) talking to the squadron commodore while we sat next to this small coastal freighter who was patiently waiting for the boarding team to come over in the morning. But it was the first one and everybody wanted it to go right."

"During Desert Shield and later Desert Storm, the pucker factor was up," says Sullivan. "Not all ships were cooperative and some had to be forced to stop and submit to inspections, either after warning shots were fired or, in extreme cases, when a SEAL team from the carrier was helicoptered over and fast-roped down to the deck. We also had intelligence, which suggested that the masters of ships flying the Iraqi flag were subject to severe punishment by Saddam Hussein if they cooperated with boarding teams. The first head over the rail of the ship after climbing a long rope ladder was extremely vulnerable to an ambush by a crew determined to resist.

"Boarding operations were conducted day and night and often in less than ideal sea conditions. Boarding teams had to negotiate rope ladders, sometimes 70 feet or more in length while carrying weapons to scale the sides of high freeboard ships. I always worried about my teams, even if the ship being boarded was cooperative; fortunately, nobody fell or got hurt.

"One night we stopped a ship coming out of the Gulf of Aqaba which had a Japanese crew. When my boarding officer got aboard and radioed back, he told me everyone was roaring drunk. It turns out that while the Japanese ship was in Aqaba, the ship's cook had died. They put him in the freezer for the trip home and then proceeded to hold a "wake" during the 100-mile trip through the Gulf of Aqaba during which everybody downed considerable amounts of sake."

"On other occasions, the job was miserable because of the conditions on the ships being boarded—Sheep carriers were the worst," recalls Sullivan. "These were large ships with nothing but cages of live sheep. They smelled awful. I was careful to position the ship upwind, but the boarding teams really stank when they came back. Our orders were to board and search every ship and that included the sheep carriers.

"I recall one occasion; Sampson stopped a ship bound for Sudan loaded with cars, trucks and buses. An Arab linguist was sent over and reported back that all the license plates, which appeared freshly painted, read 'Kuwait Province of Iraq.' These were clearly vehicles taken in Kuwait and being sold somewhere in the Sudan, another country that did not support the U.N. sanctions against Iraq," the admiral said.

As Operation Desert Shield wore on, it became obvious that the U.S. Navy needed a port in the Red Sea convenient to the intercept operations area in which to send ships for a few days rest after long, hard periods at sea. The pace was exhausting with boardings going on day and night seven days a week. The crew needed a break.

With liberty in mind, Sampson was sent to the port of Hurghada, Egypt, to determine its suitability as a rest and relaxation port.

"It sounded like a good deal at the time," says Sullivan, "but it turned into a navigation nightmare. The only chart we had of the port was an old British Admiralty chart and it didn't show any really helpful navigation aids. Those it did show, we had trouble picking out visually, once we started in. To make matters worse, the wind was blowing at around 40 knots and seas were rough. An Egyptian naval officer, who was supposed to come out to help guide us into the harbor, stayed on the pilot boat and followed us in. I finally got the ship anchored after passing between two pinnacles, which our old chart showed as being 30 feet below the surface. Our draft was 25 feet so I figured if we miscalculated on their location we'd pass safely over them with 5 feet to spare. The next day we put a boat in the water to take some soundings and discovered that the pinnacles must have grown over the years because they came to within 18 feet of the surface. When I called on the Egyptian captain of the port, I got a look at his harbor chart and the two pinnacles weren't even there! It's probably just as well that my Egyptian naval officer never got aboard because he probably would have run us right into them."

Once Operation Desert Storm began, tensions grew but in fact, according to Admiral Sullivan, ships in the Red Sea were in relatively little danger from attack because the Coalition forces dominated the skies.

"My biggest concern was still the rogue merchant ship master, particularly under an Iraqi flag, who might decide to forcibly resist my boarding team as they climbed the side of the ship. There would be little I could do without further endangering the boarding team. For that reason I always positioned the ship as close as safely possible to the ship being boarded so that we at least presented an imposing presence close at hand."

Sampson's "routine" six-month deployment to the Mediterranean ended up as a history-making eight-month deployment that carried through to the end of the war.

"I will never forget our return to Mayport with the rest of the battle group on March 28, 1991," said Sullivan. "The battle group commander, Rear Admiral Nick Gee, chose us to be the first ship into Mayport that morning. The outpouring of emotion was overwhelming. The skies were full of small aircraft and the Sea World blimp, the waters were full of boats tooting their horns and flying flags, the shoreline was lined with people waving flags and holding banners, and the tug boats were all spraying colored water. Several high school bands and groups of cheerleaders were on the piers and a general party atmosphere prevailed.

"We were truly treated to a heroes' welcome. As I drove down Mayport Road with my wife after leaving the ship that afternoon, the entire three miles was lined on both sides with people waving American flags and holding banners. It was an overwhelming experience that I will never forget."

Admiral Sullivan later returned to the Persian Gulf as skipper of the guided missile cruiser USS Cowpens (CG-63) and continued to enforce U.N. sanctions against Iraq; eight years after Sampson had conducted the first Red Sea boarding of Operation Desert Shield. "So much for those who wanted to let sanctions alone force Saddam Hussein out of Kuwait back in 1990," said Sullivan.

###

Michael Suszan:

All Jobs Equally Important

From his third floor office at the headquarters for the Chief of Naval Education and Training, Naval Air Station, Pensacola, Florida; Navy judge advocate (lawyer), Captain Michael Suszan, recalled the role he and his staff played during Operations Desert Shield/Desert Storm.

"Our normal deployment (on the USS Saratoga (CV-60) had us getting underway within days of the Iraqi invasion. I was attending the Naval War College in Newport, Rhode Island, and didn't catch up with the ship until two weeks later. I got a flight from Jiddah, Saudi Arabia, to the ship in the Red Sea," Suszan, who was a lieutenant commander at the time, said.

"I recall that personnel aboard the carrier were quite concerned about the possibility of Iraqi pilots, trained in France, using Jordanian air space to attack the ship with biological and chemical weapons.

"By the time 'Storm' kicked off, we were in a modified battle condition most of the time, which meant most of the hatches were secured. You'd have to go through the small scuttle section of the hatch to get around. GQ (general quarters) was going on all the time, along with practicing putting on gas masks."

"We had a Stinger team aboard the ship to defend us in case of attack, and SEALs to help with interdiction efforts, and of course the ship had its normal Marine detachment onboard.

"We got our news mainly through our radio feed to the BBC," Suszan recalled. "We didn't have a cable feed to CNN or anything like that. Mail call of course was a big thing. We got quite a few 'care' packages from the folks in Saratoga, New York. Stuff like toiletries and books.

"One of my concerns, as the ship's legal officer, was what to do with any enemy pilots we shot down and rescued. A lot of folks assumed that if we took a prisoner we would just lock them up in the brig. Not so.

You lock them up in the brig only if they commit a crime after being captured.

Military personnel captured during war are not criminals—just prisoners of war. You have to secure them in a place like a bunkroom with a guard. Technically, the Navy can take a prisoner of war but is obligated to turn that prisoner over to the Army. Prisoners can't be kept board ship because you'd be using them as a shield."

Suszan pointed out that another of his legal duties aboard Saratoga, was to ensure that chaplains, medical and dental personnel, performed only duties within their specialties, otherwise, they would lose their classification as non-combatants.

The primary function of the ship's legal department, according to the Navy lawyer is maintaining discipline. Suszan says that the longer a ship spends at sea the greater the number of fights, assaults, and incidents of disrespect to superior officers. "When you've been at sea for 50 days or more without a break tensions near the breaking point and the legal team has its work cut out," Suszan said.

"Right after we dropped the first bombs the executive officer told my legalmen, that we were at war and therefore all the admin stuff, we normally did, was going to be put on the back burner. 'All we're going to be doing is loading bombs and dropping bombs,' he told us. Well needless to say that without good order and discipline, everything falls apart. Our job was to see that good order and iscipline were maintained. It only took a couple of days for the XO to see the error of his ways and the legal department was back in business."

"On another occasion I recall we had a request from a pair of U.S. Army officers in Saudi Arabia who wanted to get married. In Saudi Arabia there's no recognition of Christian ceremonies, so they naturally assumed the Saratoga's commanding officer could perform a marriage onboard. That is of course a common belief, But, fact of the matter is, there's a specific prohibition against marriages aboard warships in foreign waters. Besides, the CO of an American war ship is not authorized to perform the ceremony—only a chaplain can perform weddings aboard a naval vessel."

Suszan says the saddest event he recalls from the Gulf War was the loss of 22 Saratoga crewmembers—not from combat action, but a freak accident around Christmas 1990.

"The ship was at anchor at Haifa, Israel and a ferryboat had been providing transportation between the beach and the ship. I remember that it had made a number of runs that day. Then around midnight or a little after, they were standing off waiting for another ferry to offload. When that ferry backed away, it caused enough of a motion that a wave came over and the ferry took on water real fast and sank like a rock. Most of the sailors who drowned were trapped in the interior spaces of the ferry. That was a real tragedy. To die in wartime is one thing. But to lose your shipmates in a liberty incident is real tough"

"In another incident that was a real blow to morale, I remember we heard an announcement over BBC that the Saratoga would be going home. Thinking they were going home people were on the flight deck shouting, slapping each other on the back, throwing their hats up in the air it was like a scene out of World War II. But we soon learned that was a false announcement. We weren't going anywhere near the United States. The major concern," Suszan continued, "was that once the ground war started we would be required to stay as long as everybody else. But once the ground war started, we weren't needed all that much so they (the Navy) allowed us to go home.

"The homecoming was unbelievable. The streets were lined five-thick with people on either side of the roads, and small boats waving flags in the harbor. It was easily the happiest day of our lives. My wife Polly and my two sons were part of that massive crowd of homecoming well wishers. It was just awesome."

"When I look back on that deployment and my role in the Gulf War, I realize that everybody on that ship had an important job—not just the air crews—everyone. I'm very proud of what we did aboard the ship to make it function properly," Suszan concluded.

###

Robert M. Myers:

Reckoning Recons of Saddam's War Machine

Major Robert M. Myers followed his father's lead in joining the Air Force, but his service would be a little different.

"My dad worked on airplanes," said the Austin, Texas, native. "I used to go with him on weekends when he would have to work on F-4s (Phantoms). I always thought it would be fun to fly the planes my dad worked on. I knew a lot about F-4s by the time I joined the military. It's sorta ironic— my dad worked on F-4s and I flew them."

And fly them he did during numerous reconnaissance (recon) missions during the Persian Gulf War. After receiving his navigator training and a couple of assignments, he ended up in the 12th Tactical Reconnaissance Squadron, just in time to deploy for Operation Desert Storm. In fact, Myers arrived just two days before the storm began, but getting there was miserable.

"Our deployment from the states was cancelled three nights in a row," he said. "By the third and fourth time we were set to go, the families of the squadron members just quit showing up to see us off. After a grueling trip, the squadron finally arrived at our base in southern Bahrain. We got there really, really late on Sunday and were extremely tired," he said.

"Part of the squadron flew on Monday and the (air) war kicked off on Tuesday. Basically my familiarization flight was across the Iraqi border— welcome to the war. It was routine to see AA coming up at you when you crossed the border. Some of the other personnel who had been there since right after the Iraqi invasion of Kuwait the previous August were burned out and bored and glad their war had finally started.

"The next month was a mixture of excitement and terror because we were told the survival rate for a recon squadron was pretty low, We were flying alone and unarmed, but once we got into it and it became pretty exciting and the fear, for part the most, was gone. We had a pretty good mixture of targets, looking for SAM sites and SCUDs and doing some bomb damage assessments. It never became routine. We became familiar with procedures and revisited a lot of the same targets.

"We would fly some short missions, two-three hours, over Kuwait and at other times they would be four-five hour missions up to Baghdad and over the extreme western part of Iraq. The most significant thing was flying to Baghdad and having SAMs launched at my aircraft. We'd see missiles go by and then the (F4-G) Wild Weasels shoot back at the sites,' he said.

"Early on the SAMs were the biggest fear for pilots and we knew the Weasels weren't able to kill all the sites. On one flight we let one of our cameras run long after a target pass and came up with bonus targets— SAM sites that were before unknown targets.

"As the beginning of the ground war grew closer we started looking for the Republican Guards. We had a good idea about when the ground war was going to start but not specifically until about a day or two before it kicked off.

"When it did start we were surprised about how quickly and how far the Allies advanced. Everybody was watching CNN and how their crews were reporting on Iraqis surrendering to helicopters, reporters, whatever, whomever; it was amazing! I think our thoughts at that time, were, 'how soon is this going to come to a stop?'"

Myers said that three weeks after the start of the ground war about half of his squadron returned to the states. "The rest of us stayed for awhile. The missions were pretty good because they would let us fly lower and see some of the damage more closely. Then all overland missions were stopped and it got really boring before we finally got to go home," he said.

Myers said a positive thing of his war experience was his training beforehand. "What we do is so realistic and so saturating it turned out that we were simply following training, and it works. Working together with the Navy and Marines worked out well also.

"The most negative thing I can think of is the stress; what men and women have to do when they volunteer," he said. "I don't think any of us aspire to go to war. And I know stress affected the families' back home; the worry and turmoil it put them under. But then again the outpouring of support, care packages, cards and letters from family, friends and even strangers was terrific," he concluded.

###

Dallas Smith:

Age No Barrier for Young at Heart

At 57 years of age most men have reached a point in their lives when they are beginning to give serious thought to retirement, enjoying time with the grand kids and gradually winding down from a lifetime of labor. Taking an active part in a war is the last thing on their mind. But for Summerdale, Alabama, resident Dallas Smith, the commencement of his "golden" years had an Arabian sand hue rather than a golden glow.

A first class petty officer in the naval reserve at the start of the Gulf War in 1990, Smith said he never really expected to be called to active duty. "I remember that everyone kept telling my wife, Audrey, that there was nothing to worry about. The Navy would never call a 57-year-old man up for active duty. She always replied with the same answer. 'If his unit is called up he'll be called up too.' Audrey was right. On January 16, 1991 my unit, Fleet Hospital 20 (FH-20), was activated.

"Our command master chief attended a meeting at the Philadelphia Navy Yard when hostilities broke out in 1990, and when he returned he told the unit it wasn't a matter of 'if we would be called up, but when.' In December we were ordered to Camp Pendleton (California) for additional training in fleet hospital operations."

On January 27, 1991 an advanced unit of FH-20, including Petty Officer Smith, landed in Al Jubail, Saudi Arabia, to set up Fleet Hospital 15. "It was sort of funny, really," said Smith. "We were FH-20 when we left the states and we were FH-15 when we landed in Saudi Arabia. The job of the advance unit was to get FH-15 ready for the main unit's arrival. It required a lot of work—12-14-hour days, but it was worth it. We were fully operational within 12 days," Smith said with great pride.

And proud he should be. According to a citation FH-15 received, becoming fully operational in just 12 days of arriving in theater was a Navy record for a combat zone fleet hospital. Once operational the medical staff of FH-15 took on the awesome task of caring for the medical needs of Allied troops—treating everything from tummy aches to combat wounds.

The primary task for Petty Officer Smith and his small band of storekeepers for the remainder of the Gulf War was to try and keep the hospital supplied.

"We were a fully self-contained organization," said Smith. "In addition to the medical staff, we had admin personnel, supply personnel and a Seabee unit. In many respects the long hours were a welcome aversion from the even longer hours of boredom. There wasn't any liberty to speak of because there was no place to go. There certainly wasn't any alcohol available in Saudi Arabia. So we spent most of our off-duty time writing letters, listening to music, playing games, and having our picture taking with a camel. We did have one opportunity to go to Bahrain for liberty, where alcohol was legal in the America compound, and do a little shopping."

The cessation of hostilities forced the cancellation of a second Bahrain liberty, according to Smith, because all hands were needed to dismantle the hospital and prepare to return home. "Not surprisingly, no one complained about having their liberty cancelled." Smith smiled.

Smith actually returned home a couple of weeks earlier than most of his shipmates.

"My son was graduating from college... a ceremony that just a few weeks before, I didn't think I would be able to attend. So when the war ended I put in a request to leave on the first flight out. I figured that after putting out all that money to put my boy through college it would be nice to be there to see him graduate," Smith laughed. "My request was approved and I left Saudi Arabia April 21, 1991. The rest of my storekeepers got home around May 10."

Like other Gulf War units, the men and women of FH-15 arrived home to a hero's welcome. Many of the Gulf War veterans were later given special recognition by their individual hometowns and veterans organizations. Smith says that while he doesn't recommend going to war at 57 years of age, he would be willing to do it again if called upon.

What did his wife think about her husband going to war at such an advanced age?

"I wasn't worried. He had been in the service for a good number of years and I knew he could take care of himself," Audey said.

Petty Officer Smith retired from the Naval Reserve one month and 28 days after reaching his 60th birthday in 1993.

###

Pride, Confidence
<u>Replace Fear, Anxiety</u>

*A decade after the Persian Gulf War, three Gulf War veterans—
Master Chief Petty Officer Wallace Morris, Petty Officer First Class
Kenneth Butler and Petty Officer First Class Tony Dicapo—all former
members of Navy Attack Squadron Seventy-Two (VF-72) based at Naval
Air Station Cecil Field, near Jacksonville, Florida, were reunited at their
new duty station, Naval Air Station, Pensacola, Florida.*

*The three squadron mates were asked to recount their Gulf War expe-
riences for a newspaper article. At the time, Morris and Dicapo were
assigned to the Navy's Flight Demonstration Squadron, the Blue Angels,
and Butler was assigned to the Pensacola Naval Air Station Public Affairs
Office.*

*Each sailor's experience was different, yet they were the same. Each
had left a family back home, each had some fear of what lay ahead and
each were filled with anxieties.*

*Each also knew that pride and confidence in their country and their Navy
replaced any anxiety they felt. These are their stories.*

Wallace Morris

One Friday in August 1990, Scott and Benjamin Morris received
some disappointing news—their dad, Senior Chief Wallace Morris,
would sail the following Monday aboard the USS Kennedy (CV-67)
as the night check maintenance control chief for VA-72.

"VA-72 was in the process of standing down. We were going to
trade our A-7 Corsair IIs for A/F-18 Hornets and we had given up
all but seven of the Corsairs, Morris said. "That Friday afternoon we
took possession of five new A-7s, did all the acceptance inspections
on them, field carrier landing practice qualified all of our pilots,
packed up all of our gear, put it on trucks, and sent it to Norfolk,
Virginia, to be loaded aboard the Kennedy. The Kennedy was
planning to "steam around" for about six weeks to be prepared to
go to the Middle East if the United States became involved in a
war. Morris said, "In reality, we got qualified, sat for about five days

191

and they pushed the button and said, 'Alright, you're going.' So we went non-stop through the Suez Canal. We made it into the Red Sea, but we never actually got into the Persian Gulf.

"Because we had A-7s, we had a longer range than the A/F-18s, so they left us in the Red Sea. In fact, VA-72 and VA-46 were the last two A-7 Corsair II units to fly in combat. After the carrier group arrived in the Red Sea, we simply waited for something to happen. Our biggest fear was that Saddam might launch one of those Scud missiles at us. The first time they did fire Scuds into Saudi Arabia the general feeling aboard ship was 'Oh, my God, we're next.'

"The most memorable point of the whole thing was when the ships that were in our battle group fired Tomahawk missiles at night," Morris remembers. "You're sitting there watching and all of a sudden you see little missile blooms everywhere and it's like, 'Oh, boy, here we go.'"

Morris explained that soon after the missile launches began, the aircrews began an around the clock firefight. "We were putting from seven to nine A-7s in the air at one time. They would be away for six, maybe seven hours at a time, catching tankers (refueling in the air) on the way in and out. They'd get back, we'd recover them, turn around what we could and launch a second strike and then fix the rest of them, so that the next day, at roughly the same time, we could put another seven to nine planes in the air.

"The A-7s were flying from the Red Sea all the way to Baghdad—that's a long-range hit," Morris said. He said the daily routine became a blur of repetition. He recounts one particular flight that was different from the others, however.

"On this one particular launch, something happened that caused one of the nose tires to sheer off during the launch. The pilot came back around and had to dump all his ordnance and fuel tanks. They brought him back aboard and trapped him in a barricade. The act of trapping the plane in the barricade broke the plane in half. We took the aircraft down to the hangar deck and stripped it and saved every useful part we could.

"We then took the airplane back up on the flight deck, had a big ceremony and shoved it over the side. To show you how obstinate an A-7 can be, it took three tries before they could shove that tough old bird over the side. It just refused to go. It kept tangling up its landing gear in the safety nets on the side of the ship. And then when they finally got it in the water, it refused to sink.

Finally the ship's captain brought the Marines out on deck with .50-caliber machine guns and they shot it full of holes so it would sink. I tell you, it was the darnest thing, that old war bird just absolutely refused to die."

In looking back, I would have to say that it was pretty much a standard cruise," says Morris, "except that we were dropping live ordnance. The planes were leaving full and coming back with the racks empty; other than that, it was pretty much a standard thing. From our standpoint, we had a lot less interaction with foreign forces during the Gulf War than you do in a regular deployment. The Russian Bears weren't overflying us and we didn't have to track Russian submarines.

With that many aircraft carriers floating around I guess the Russians decided it might be best if they remained clear of the area. Personally, I pulled my hair out trying to keep the airplanes up, and the day the shooting stopped, they sent me home," Morris 'smiled. "Pretty routine stuff."

Kenneth O. Butler

Petty Officer Second Class Kenneth O. Butler was a jet mechanic assigned to the Blue Hawks of VA-72. While the squadron was conducting workups onboard the USS John F. Kennedy, Butler had been granted permission to stay behind in Jacksonville because his wife was expecting their third child.

But Butler's home stay was short lived. He got to see his son born, but after only a few weeks with the newborn, Butler and VA-72 put to sea where they spent the next seven months preparing for and engaging in war.

"The squadron was transitioning from A-7s to the A/F-18 and in early August I was attending a weeklong indoctrination training course on the A/F-18," said the Ladson, S.C., native. "When the course was about over, we decided to have a graduation party. It was at the party that I got word that the squadron would be leaving.

"Before I got back to Jacksonville, the squadron called my wife and told her I was to report in at 0600 (6 a.m.) the next day, which was Saturday. When I reported in I found out the squadron was getting all the Corsairs back. We were to conduct acceptance inspections and prepare to leave for Norfolk on Monday for deployment aboard the Kennedy. We were also told that there was a good possibility we could be going to war with Iraq.

The Iraqi invasion of Kuwait had taken place almost two weeks before the Kennedy departed Norfolk.

"We floated around for awhile out in the Atlantic until our aircraft flew aboard then we headed south. As we neared South Carolina more aircraft came aboard. Then we picked up speed and headed for the Mediterranean. The transit across the Atlantic was one of speed once all the aircraft were onboard and chained down

"I didn't really know if we were going to war or not, but, like everyone aboard, I knew there was that possibility. Like many other people aboard the Kennedy—though they wouldn't admit it—I was a little scared. We didn't know what kind of weapons Iraq had or whether or not their weapons could even reach us. But we knew we had to go; we had an obligation to go.

"On the way across most things were routine. Others were a little unusual. We pulled a lot of drills that were normal, but we also went through a lot of chemical, biological and radiological (CBR) warfare drills. Those drills were first conducted on a scheduled basis and then they became surprise drills. If we were asleep and a CBR drill started, we had to get up, report to our shop with chemical gear and actively participate. Those unscheduled drills produced a lot of tired, sleepy people. After a while it became a safety issue because of the lack of sleep.

"The normal work shifts were long and tiring enough. Some of us worked more than 12 hours a day," Butler recalls. "Even though everyone knew the drills were important, it was hard to try and thoroughly participate. Once command thought we had the drills down pat and knew how to react in the event of a CBR attack, the safety factor was taken into consideration and they let people sleep in.

It took the Kennedy about 10 days to get on station in the Mediterranean. Once there we started to do flight operations for practice; doing different training exercises for the pilots to keep them proficient but also to get them comfortable. Being thrown on a ship like we were and possibly heading to war didn't give the pilots much time to get comfortable," Butler said.

The Kennedy and its carrier battle group eventually moved into the Red Sea where flight operations continued. Over the next several weeks, training continued as the sailors and marines embarked and waited for word of war. We were told the morning of January 17 (1991) that we would be launching for real that night, or early the next morning. That night I was talking to one of the pilots that would be going. I knew him pretty well and I could see it in his eyes; he was scared to death," said Butler.

"We were in the passageway outside the Quality Assurance shop (where Butler was assigned) and I was talking to him about it. I said, 'Look, this is what you've been trained for. You've trained for this your entire naval career. I'd be scared too if I had to go do what you have to do, but this is what you've trained for and you'll be out there laying down bombs. We talked for a little while longer and I finally just told him everything was going to be fine and I'd see him when he got back. I think that made him feel little better.

"When he got back relief showed in his eyes. He had completed his first mission of the war and he lived through it," said Butler. "And he made it through the whole thing."

"Around midnight other ships begin firing Tomahawks and it looked like fireworks. They shot Tomahawks for about an hour. We were getting our planes ready to launch. I was the safety observer and we had a lot of people that wanted to be on the flight deck to see the first launch. But for their own safety, everyone who was not essential had to leave.

"There was a sense of eagerness to get the planes off the deck; a sense of pride and confidence that our planes would be coming back, and at 0120 (1:20 a.m.), the first ones took off.

"Everyone was excited to be part of the historic event. There was a lot of smiling faces on the flight deck that night. Happy that they were part of it. These were our aircraft being launched to go bomb this guy who had invaded another country.

"From there, we conducted round-the-clock launches going through the cycles of sending them off and recovering them," said Butler. "Within the next few days we saw a piece of video footage from a Slam missile with a camera in the nose going into an Iraqi building. That missile was from one of our aircraft. That was seen on TV over and over, all over the world.

"Even though there was a war going on a lot of things were still routine: going to the barbershop, eating, going to the gym and library on what little off-time we had," he said. "We still had CBR drills going on because at first we didn't know the range of the Iraqi missiles and what they were loaded with. We were told later that we (the battle group) were fired on with Scud missiles, but they had fallen 300 miles short in Saudi Arabia, never even getting close.

"When we were told the ground war was about to start we had been bombing for more than a month and we figured there wasn't going to be much to it because so much had already been destroyed. And there wasn't much to it. It only took 100 hours, but there was still a lot of relief when we heard it was over. And when we were told we were going home... wow! Everyone on that that ship, and probably the whole battle group, was happy, laughing—just overjoyed.

"When we arrived back home there were thousands of people waiting for us. The only thing I wanted to do was get to my family and when I found them it was the happiest moment of my life. It was something that words will never be able to explain."

Petty Officer Butler retired from the Navy in March 2002 after 20 years of active duty.

Tony Dicapo

Tony Dicapo, who at the time was a 23-year-old avionics technician assigned to VA-72, echoed Morris' comments about the Kennedy's 1991 deployment being routine.

"Other than the fact that there was a madman named Saddam Hussein on the loose and the planes took off with bombs and returned without them, it was just another day at the office— troubleshooting communication and navigational systems on A-7 Corsairs"

It's just that Dicapo's "office" happened to be in the middle of the Red Sea and the Persian Gulf War. For sure, it was an awful long way from Lawrenceburg, Tenn., where he'd enlisted in the Navy in 1986, looking for a stable job with educational and travel opportunities.

Dicapo recalled a typical day aboard Kennedy during Operation Desert Shield meant training followed by firefighting drills, followed by medical casualty drills, general quarters, and naval exercises with the battle group and other world navies. Special attention was also paid to proper procedures in case of a chemical or biological attack by Iraq.

"We were putting in 16-hour days," recalls Dicapo. I clearly recall the moment that the Carrier Group Two commander (Rear Adm. Riley Mixson) announced over the intercom... 'We're bombing tonight.' It was 1:20 in the morning, the date was January 17, 1991," says Dicapo.

"I was working days at the time. I woke up at 1 a.m., looked at my watch and heard the planes turning up. I remember thinking and saying to myself, 'Oh wow! Here it is—we're about to attack the place we've been talking about for the last five months.' That was a weird feeling."

"During those months I slept one deck below the flight deck—I never really got used to it—I literally didn't sleep for the first few nights. Eventually, though, I got so tired that I could've slept just about anywhere. I'd try to relax with a visit to the library or one of the gyms—great way to relieve stress," Dicapo laughed.

"It's really amazing that with all of the sorties we didn't have one casualty—that'd be a great statistic even on a regular deployment. When we left (Norfolk) we really had no idea when we'd be coming back," says Dicapo.

When the Kennedy arrived back in Norfolk on March 28, 1991, Dicapo's mom was among the more than 50,000 other proud Americans waiting pier-side for the Kennedy to dock.

"I never once give any thought to the fact that I might not be coming home. I felt safe. I knew what the ship and her crew were capable of doing. I was pretty confident. And when it was all over," he smiles, "I had a feeling of accomplishment—a feeling of pride."

###

Danny Scott:

A Line in the Sand

He arrived in Al Jebel on November 13, 1990, as a corpsman serving with the Marine Corps' 2nd Fleet Service Support Group (FSSG). Danny Scott ended up serving with 13 different units, including Marine reconnaissance, during his eight months in the Middle East.

"I bounced around a lot. I don't know how they got my name," Scott says. "I was just a field medic corpsman, but different commands kept asking for me. So, I was with Lima Company, Combat Skills Company, I did a stint with EOD (Explosive Ordnance Disposal), an MP Company, Ammo Company and the 6th Marines. I also served some time with British troops."

Oftentimes Scott would not only fulfill his duties as a corpsman, but stepped into the shoes of a Marine who had been injured and complete that Marine's duties.

If someone got hurt, I had to fill in," Scott said. Laughing, he added, "It was fun at the time, it was great at the time, but now that I look back, I ask myself, 'Would I do that now? Spiral rigging, fast roping, and jumping out of moving helicopters and hitting the water. I'm too old for that stuff, now... but it was fun at the time."

Before the war actually began, according to Scott, the troops were given time off after building bunkers and ensuring the area was safe in case of chemical attack. He explained that the troops had their picture taken while playing volleyball and the picture ended up on the cover of Time magazine. A short time later we came across another group of journalists being briefed on what they were allowed to write. They were told that nothing could be sent without first being approved by a military PAO (public affairs officer). That included text, video and photographs.

"One of the journalists protested and said something like, 'You can't do that. Our rights as American journalists are protected by the Constitution.' One of the officers looked straight at the journalist and said, 'Look, this is a time of war. If you release anything without permission, we will consider that an act of treason. And in war time the penalty for treason is death.' The guy looked at him and said, 'You can't do that.' And, I remember this distinctly. The officer unclipped his side arm and said, 'Don't test my resolve. Don't you be the first.'

Scott said that he recalls talking with a fellow corpsman, Mark Ware, and telling Ware about a dream he had had. According to his dream something bad was going to happen to their unit.

I remember telling Ware that although in my dream it was really bad, I certainly didn't think it was actually going to happen. Ware asked me for an explanation and I told him that according to the dream whatever was going to happen would take place that night. It's really bad and there's a chance that many of us could all die if it happens the way it happened in the dream."

"What about me?" Ware asked.

"You're going to be fine," I told him.

"What about you?"

"I don't know about me. I just don't know."

Ware asked Scott if he was psychic and Scott said no, it was just a dream.

"About an hour later, a 7th Cav tank division came shooting across the desert. There must have been about 30 tanks and they were really moving. A staff sergeant told me that an Iraqi tank division had attempted to attack the 7th Cav but had overshot their mark. The sergeant said the 7th Cav was now chasing the Iraqi tanks. Had the Iraqis not overshot their mark, our unit would have been overrun because 7th Cav would not have been able to get to us in time."

"Ware said, "Man, I'm going to stick by you all the time. You know what's going on. I've got to hang with you.' He (Ware) told everybody, I mean everybody. Sometime after that is when I started leapfrogging to different units. I had three sea bags. I would keep two with me and leave one behind."

While with Direct Support Group Forward (DSG) on the main service road, which led into Kuwait, Scott was the only medical person available to the units along a 100-mile stretch of roadway. Scott said he was told there had been an accident and he needed to go. So, he grabbed his "beach bag" (medical bag) and raced to the scene.

"They were driving LSDs (tanker trucks)," Scott said. "They were driving in a convoy and following each other too close. One truck stopped and there was so much dirt and dust the drivers couldn't see. One truck ran into the back of the one that had stopped. A third truck hit and when it did they 'fireballed.'

"By the time I got there the trucks were completely burned. I looked at one of the Marines lying on the ground and he grabbed my leg. Out of reaction I snatched my leg back.

"Scotty, he started saying, 'don't let me die.' Who are you? I asked. He was burned so badly I couldn't recognize him. I tried to take care of him, but there wasn't really much I could do. I looked at his boot and I saw a dog tag. That shook me up real bad, because I knew him. The guys who drove me out there (there were six of us) were all vomiting. I said, 'Look, man, I don't have time for this. Y'all have got to help me. If you don't, these guys are going to die."

Scott eventually got through to them and the men pitched in and did whatever Scott asked. Knowing that he needed a flight surgeon, Scott grabbed a radio. In spite of the red tape, a heated argument, and a threat to shoot the radio operator on the other end, Scott was able to have a flight surgeon aboard the helicopter he had requested. When the surgeon arrived, Scott explained to him that he had cut the men in order to find a vein to insert IV needles.

According to Scott, the surgeon said, "This guy's burnt too bad. He can't breathe. I have to cut his chest because it's crusted over, and his chest can't rise and fall. He's suffocating."

"We got him on the bird (helicopter) and he (flight surgeon) starts cutting him." Scott said. When he finally cut all the way through you could hear a whoosh and the guy took a real deep breath."

Two of the Marines were severely burned. A lance corporal, whose truck was hauling JP-5, was burned over more than 90 percent of his body. He didn't survive. A second lance corporal, which did survive, was burned over more than 60 percent of his body and lost a leg because of the accident.

"Yeah, I remember those guys. They were my friends."

# # #

Steve Whitcomb:

<u>Clash of the Titans</u>

As the second month of the 1990 hurricane season settled upon the Gulf Coast, Pensacola, Florida residents were casually listening to the latest weather reports. It had been more than a decade since a major storm had unleashed its fury on the Pensacola area and early predictions indicated that 1990 would be another mild year for storm activity.

Half a world away, however, storm clouds of another kind were forming over the Middle East and Lieutenant Colonel Steve Whitcomb, was about to get drenched.

In a public statement on July 17, 1990, Iraqi President Saddam Hussein accused Kuwait of plotting with the United States to keep oil prices low and vowed to take matters in his own hands. Two weeks later, August 2, 1990, Hussein positioned troops and tanks along the Kuwaiti border. Over the next several days the storm clouds gathering over the Arabian landscape grew ever more ominous.

Whitcomb, commanding officer of the Army's 1st Armored Division, 2nd Battalion, 70th Armor Task Force, based in Germany, was instructed to shift his focus from defense (of Europe) to deployment. Little did the future general realize that within a few weeks he would be engaged in a modern day "Clash of the Titans."

The son of a naval aviator, Whitcomb said he initially wanted to go to the Naval Academy and follow his father, retired Commander Roy Whitcomb, into naval aviation.

"My eyes weren't good enough to fly and there wasn't anything else I wanted to do in the Navy, so I gave up on the academy and accepted a football scholarship to the University of Virginia."

In addition to football, the University of Virginia also gave the naval aviator's son his first taste of Army life. "It was never my intention to make the Army a career when I joined the Army ROTC unit. I really never expected to stay in the Army for more than a couple of years."

203

But stay he did, and on December 27, 1990, Whitcomb's command deployed for Saudi Arabia.

"When our tanks, trucks and other gear arrived we made some modifications to the tanks and repainted them from the traditional green color to sand. We also had to off-load our ammunition from ships and reload it into the tanks. So those first few days were very busy," Whitcomb recalls. "Saddam also launched the first SCUD missiles during that time.

According to the intelligence we had received, the Iraqi Army was reportedly the fourth or fifth largest army in the world. We believed them to be well trained and well equipped. They had recently fought a war with Iran and we knew they had used chemical weapons against Iran. So we didn't know what to expect."

The ground war kicked off at 4 a.m. February 24, 1991. Whitcomb's command made its first contact with the enemy at a town called Al Busayyah, a large logistics base protected by a well dug-in Iraqi commando unit.

"We came upon the unit at night so we pulled up about 15 miles from the town and prepared to attack the next morning. At first light, about 0700 (7a.m.) we attacked with an infantry battalion on my left and my tank battalion on the right. There was some stiff resistance at first, but the Iraqis were quickly overrun.

"I can tell you that the Iraqi commandos weren't a force to be taken lightly. Unlike many units of the Iraqi army who were totally outclassed, the commandos wouldn't quit. So we had to kill them," Whitcomb said nonchalantly.

"After taking the town of Al Busayyah we continued our push to the north. Our first clash with the enemy had been extremely successful. We captured 16 enemy soldiers and destroyed numerous vehicles including seven tanks, and 25 wheeled vehicles. Although the Iraqi commando units and the Republican Guard were powerful adversaries the regular army didn't gain much respect.

"Our biggest fight of the war—actually the largest tank battle since World War II—occurred next to the last day of the ground war. I remember that it was around 1700, when a large concentration of enemy tanks was reported moving northwest. The division commander assessed that the Republican Guards were withdrawing, and ordered us to 'press them to the wall.'

"At 0140 on the morning of February 27, we were alerted that the task force would be engaging a brigade of the Adnan Republican Guards division. At 0700, the report 'tanks, direct front, engaging now' came over the radio.

"The task force encountered what proved to be a Republican Guard headquarters or supply unit. There was little enemy resistance but we did engage a truck loaded with a combustible material which exploded—releasing clouds of yellow smoke. The brigade commander immediately ordered the company to turn on the overpressure systems on the tanks as they passed through the fumes. Fortunately, it was not a chemical agent.

"Decisive and methodical, the task force overran the objective with well-placed fire," Whitcomb recalled. "We destroyed eight tanks, 11 BMPs, three BRDMs, and 34 trucks. We also captured at least 30 Iraqi prisoners."

"After taking the objective the task force moved forward about six kilometers then halted to reorganize, consolidate, and prepare for future operations. It was the fourth and final conflict of the war," said Whitcomb. "The task force had participated in the largest U.S. armored operation since World War II.

"We moved faster than (German Field Marshal) Rommel and further than (U.S. General) Patton to strike deep, carrying the battle into the enemy's homeland. Focusing deliberate and violent fire into an irresistible force of destruction, we swept the enemy from the battlefield, leaving the remnants of his army in ruins. It was a clash of titans—a clash which we won."

After the cease-fire Whitcomb and his unit moved into Kuwait to secure the border. Only then, did he realize the extent of the senseless devastation caused by the Iraqis.

"At one point I could see 37 oils rigs burning. That was just senseless devastation. There was just no reason for it," says, Whitcomb. While there can be little doubt that Whitcomb is proud of his role in the cash of the titans, the thing he is most proud of is the fact all of his troops returned home. "I was very fortunate," he says with a satisfied grin, "that I was able to bring all my troops home alive."

###

Brian M. Kane:

The Hundred-Hour War

Brian M. Kane wanted to be an officer. After graduating from the University of Florida in 1986, he enlisted in the U.S. Army with the intent of going to Officer Candidate School (OCS). After three years as an enlisted man, he finally made it.

After completing OCS and receiving his commission as a second lieutenant in the U.S. Army, the Cleveland, Ohio, native completed intelligence officer training and was then assigned to Honduras for a brief time. Following the Honduras detail he was reassigned to the 2nd Brigade, 1st Armored Division in Europe.

"I received orders on August 5, 1990 (three days after the invasion of Kuwait). My wife was ecstatic because I would be in Germany where it was safe," Kane recalls.

But that was about to change. When Kane arrived in Germany, he ran all the Iraq Intel for the brigade commander. "Iraq wasn't a topic we had discussed before but that's what I was handed when I got there," he said. "I was briefing the brigade on threat weapons and familiarization with Iraq and the Middle East.

"My family had not even arrived in Europe yet," he said. "My wife had a baby July 26, 1990, and wasn't able to travel yet." And I was tagged to be on the brigade's advance party heading to the Middle East. I'll admit, I was nervous."

By the time November rolled around the buildup in the desert was underway. It was reported on the TV show "Good Morning America" that 7th Corps (under which the 1st Armored Division fell) was going to Desert Storm. "My wife had only recently arrived in Germany and saw it on TV before word was supposed to go out."

The advance party was told they would be leaving soon. "I kept telling my wife 'we're leaving tomorrow; we're leaving Thursday.' My wife was going nuts. Finally, a few weeks later, they called the advance party off and the brigade left en masse. We arrived in Saudi

December 22 or 23 at a big tent city where in-processing was conducted," he said.

"By New Year's we were out of the tent city and were sent to middle-of nowhere Saudi Arabia," said Kane. "My captain, another lieutenant and I, were all tracking the Iraqi positions and setting up the threat situation and scenarios for the ground war.

"So, we're sitting in Saudi Arabia and early on the morning of January 17, I'm manning the radio and hear that the Tomahawks are being fired. I woke up the colonel and said, 'Sir, it's started.'

But Kane and his fellow soldiers were confident. "We had a very competent and confident staff. I remember sending taped messages to my wife saying if I had be someplace I'd rather be here surrounded by these tanks because they're the toughest in the world.

"Within about three or four hours of notifying the colonel we had 'jumped,' we picked up all our pieces (tanks, Bradleys, APCs, trucks and personnel) and moved them to an undisclosed location somewhat closer to the Iraqi border awaiting further orders. We continued to jump every few days so the enemy wouldn't know where we were."

That went on for more than a month while the air war was being waged. During that time Kane was assigned as the assistant brigade intelligence officer, briefing battalion commanders and the brigade colonel. "For the first three weeks of February we were running Intel briefs for the commanders; no breaks, no relief, every day.

"On about February 22, the brigade commander said he wanted 'eyes out front.' Me, being 2nd Lt. Kane, the lowest-ranking officer in his command group, and an Intel officer, I was selected to find a vehicle, a driver, and three radios to go out in front of the brigade when it rolled forward. I was ecstatic."

Kane found a driver and two flak jackets, one to wear and one to sit on in case the vehicle detonated a land mine. But he and his driver sergeant had not secured a vehicle or the radios because everyone was holding on to their own equipment. "I went back to the colonel and told him, 'Sir, no one's coughing them up.'

"Well, then we immediately got a vehicle (a humvee) and radios, but the vehicle was one that someone else had DX'd (turned in for repair or stripped for parts). We got some 100-mph tape (duct tape) and taped the windshield because it was cracked. I had to use a Coke can for a gas cap. But I did have three good radios."

Kane's unit wasn't set to jump off for the now-famous left flank end- round maneuver until February 25, but the initial ground contact and breaching of Iraqi sand berms were going more smoothly than originally anticipated. So, the ground war began a day early, on February 24.

"Back in October or November, we had a meeting with our division G2 (Intel) and we discussed theoretically the end-round run for Desert Storm, but it was strictly theory then and was not to be broadcast. Then in January, we saw it published in some magazine, I believe it was *Time*, as a possible operation when the ground war started."

"Because of the early success of the ground campaign, the brigade's time table was moved up to jump off. My sergeant and I had to find the brigade because we were already out and all alone. We found them and rolled forward with them, but we were still out front," he said. "Our DX'd humvee broke down everywhere, but it made it through the war."

Kane said because the brigade moved out early, things were packed quickly. There was a stove that was put in a trailer behind one of the brigade's operations vehicles. The trailers were used to carry spare equipment, duffel bags and other items. "The stove was still hot and caught on fire. I remember watching the trailer burning up as we were driving along. One of our operations officers lost everything, uniforms, everything," he chuckled, "But we couldn't stop."

"The first day was strictly driving through fierce sandstorms. We couldn't see anything. We drove into the night. My sergeant and I were on our own the first night because we were out front. I pulled guard duty while he slept," said Kane. "And stupid me, I had a pistol and he had an M-16. I didn't think to borrow his M-16. I was standing out there with a pistol.

"On the morning of the 25th around 4 a.m., I saw a huge MLRS (multiple-launch rocket system) barrage go off. "There must have been a full battery firing; it was phenomenal. Then we launched forward and made our first Iraqi contact at Al Busayyah.

"Those guys would not come out of their bunkers. They would not leave and they would not give up. They were firing at us so we had to go in and kill them.

"On the 26th we ran into heavy fire from tanks, mortars and machine guns," he said. "It was part of the Republican Guard. The Air Force came in with A-10s; that was the coolest thing I've ever seen. Remember, I was in a Humvee and not very well protected. We watched the A-10s take out the enemy tanks. That felt good.

"At one point we could tell a lot of the Iraqis wanted to give up, but there were others, their own guys, who shot them," said Kane. "There was an escaping truck with a machine gun on back that was shooting at other Iraqis. One of our tanks put a round into the truck.

"The next day, the 27th, we hit the Republican Guard in force; B Brigade of the Adnan Republican Guard. That was our biggest tank-on-tank battle (the biggest anywhere since World War II). Their tanks didn't have the range ours had," he said. "We were hitting theirs and their rounds were falling short of us landing in the dirt. It was a very controlled battle for us."

The Adnan Republican Guard was considered one of Saddam Hussein's best units. But with only 200 rounds fired from 2nd Brigade's tanks and TOWs from its Bradley fighting vehicles and supporting Apache helicopters, 160 enemy tanks were destroyed in the 40-minute engagement.

"The Iraqis had some of their tanks buried up to the turret. Those that weren't destroyed were still running. The engines were on so they were coming up 'hot' on our thermals," he said. "We didn't know if they were going to fire on us or surrender...we couldn't tell. As it turned out, most had fled their tanks and left them running.

210

"A friend of mine, another Intel officer from another battalion, got selected to go out and turn off the tanks. Luckily, they weren't booby- trapped," said Kane.

"Then we saw a lot of the Iraqis leaving en masse and wanted to pursue them but we were told to halt and wait for further instructions. The next morning (February 28) we were already rolling forward but were told to stop because the cease-fire had gone into effect," he said. "Unfortunately, we were only a few kilometers away from the town of Basra. We sat in place for several days while getting reports that Iraqis were killing civilians there. They were part of an uprising against Saddam Hussein. We had all this armor and we were not allowed to proceed. It was frustrating."

Even though the cease-fire had been implemented, Kane was still busy. "I did Intel runs, going out to see bunkers. There were bunkers with furniture; stereos; office equipment; maps; Korans, some the size of matchbooks; and even what appeared to be chemical weaponry. It was noted that some of the chemical materials were from countries that were not supposed to be supplying the Iraqis.

"At one point I had to go out and identify an armored ambulance. The Iraqis had machine guns on top of their ambulances," he said. "When I got to the location where the battalion had spotted the vehicle, one of our company commanders came chasing me down in his tank. I was in my Humvee and he told me that I shouldn't get any closer because there was a minefield. So he took me to the ambulance in his tank to photograph it for division Intel.

"In some of the other things I was recording, I found 'unprepared' Iraqi equipment," said Kane. "They had plastic ponchos to act as biological and chemical protective gear. It made me feel good because I don't think they would have launched chemical weapons without having decent protective equipment. Their helmets weren't really helmets at all. They were more like helmet liners from our old steel pots. We thought that was kind of funny," he said. "We were very shocked by their lack of equipment and capability they had."

When Kane's unit redeployed back into Saudi Arabia into a tent city, they got a treat. They had not had hot water since arriving in theater. For the first five weeks of the war, there was no showering or bathing at all. Water was far too precious in the desert

"We came home to very little fanfare, there really wasn't much noise at all," he said. "We were amazed to see all the parades and welcome home celebrations back in the states. But it was OK, we did our job."

###

Irene Tichelaar:

Desert Storm Diary

In August 1990 Lieutenant Commander Irene Tichelaar, assigned to U.S. Central Command (CENTCOM) J-4 Logistics Branch in Tampa, Florida, was attending a joint logistics conference at Holloman Air Force Base, New Mexico. The previous day attendees had been briefed on an operation plan, which specified a country invading Kuwait from the north.

During the first morning's briefing a colonel stated that though the plan had assumed such an action would take 10 days, Iraq had in fact invaded Kuwait, and in one day.

"We were to pack our bags and head home to Tampa, where I was charged with management of pre-positioned material," she said. "The next few weeks were spent releasing the pre-positioned material and arranging for its movement to the theater of operation," remembers Tichelaar.

"Additionally, the staff worked on the deployment of the armed forces and accompanying military material. The entire staff was dressed in the desert camouflage uniform to show support for the deployed troops."

The following are direct quotes from letters Tichelaar sent to friends and family, and from a personal diary she kept.

September 13, 1990—My friends tease me by saying I have become a "lady of the evening," working 6 p.m.-6 a.m. This puts me in line with Saudi time where the vast majority of our headquarters have moved. My current deployment status (or lack thereof) is a result of the command's sensitivities to the Saudi position regarding the place of women in their society. Saudi women are not allowed to drive, take public transportation, eat in restaurants, or walk down the street with a man other than their husband. (These same rules would later apply to female military members. The women that first deployed at the HQ in Saudi were not treated as professional equals by the Saudi military members, for example, being required to enter the HQ building via the back door).

213

In early December I received three days notice to pack my duffel bag and be ready to go. After arranging for someone to stay in my apartment, stored my car, updated my will and got multiple shots I was on my way to "somewhere in Saudi Arabia in the vicinity of Riyadh." As the pre-positioned material was now in place in country, our J-4 team focused on continued support of the deploying troops; working 12 on, 12 off, seven days a week. The most vivid memories or those of the overwhelming support we received from family, friends and strangers back home—particularly during the Christmas holidays.

We lived in an apartment complex owned by the Lockheed Corporation. Six women shared a small two-bedroom apartment where I "hot-bunked" on a cot with a Navy Reserve nurse who was working days.

Religious celebrations were "social support meetings" and the chaplains were called "morale officers," again in deference to Saudi Muslim traditions. But we did have a Santa Claus crawl in the basement recreation room window, dressed in camouflage with a mop wig and beard. And we were treated to visits from numerous stars and the Bob Hope show (less any female performers).

January 17, 1991—Admittedly humor gets rather warped under stress. On the 15th CNN news programming was termed the pre-game show. The J-4 general came in to give us an update; i.e., lead the pep-rally. I was chosen homecoming queen, and our chemical protective gear is being considered our game jerseys. We woke to the sounds of multiple planes warming up and heading north. The liberation of Kuwait had begun.

January 21—Six launches of SCUD missile into Saudi Arabia... brings to mind "the rockets' red glare." (Some of) the rockets were the Patriot missiles fired in response. Repeated alerts as the B-52s strike launch sites. That's OK, SPACECOM (Space Command) is doing their job.

January 24—It was amazing to watch CNN during the bombing. And ironically during the initial SCUD attacks we watched TV to find out what was going one.

January 25—(letter) I know it may be hard to understand that I'm glad to be here. First, I'm doing what I was trained to do, provide support, to those fighting for continued freedom in this world. Secondly, in the sense that I know [now] what is happening to my friends here and know you my family and friends are safe at home.

January 27—CNN quoted one of the troops: "We will be on the edge of our seats no matter how exciting the (Super Bowl) game." Ironically we were able to watch the game because we had been awakened by another SCUD attack and chemical alarm.

January 29—It truly is a "small world after all"; keep running into friends I have served with elsewhere. Interesting comment from one: "Hope you're keeping a diary."

January 31—Received a letter from Rev. Harwell (St. Petersburg) reporting that at the exact moment the air war started the church started a vigil for me. He had a premonition that I needed those prayers.

February 1—The war must be slowing down, CNN is showing David Letterman and Johnny Carson. This lack of action is actually disconcerting. If Saddam's intent is psychological pressure, it is having some effect. Casualty reports reflecting "adjustment disorder" or depression and anxiety. That's my greatest fear—being sent home as "unfit for combat."

February 20—(letter) We decided this war is going to be won by charts (because the Japanese could not provide troops we have each been given a computer, and electronic entertainment equipment in our residences). Every question now seems to require a briefing chart. Despite the fact that I answer the phone "War sustainability" sometimes it's hard to realize there is a war going on. But then I am reminded all too vividly as I listen to the Joint Mortuary Affairs Office personnel sitting in our office.

As others have found before me, the war experience can significantly change you. Already in two months I have grown emotionally and spiritually. There's an unprecedented openness in the office—a willingness to share feelings, both positive and negative, vent frustrations, give praise, etc. Walls are breaking down, friendships bonded. As my pastor predicted I have become the surrogate mother, wife or sister. In the case of our "group," I wouldn't have made it without the support of my "brothers." Even the teasing is healing. We will never be the same.

March 7—(letter) Assalaamu alayku: Peace be upon you. This is the standard Arabic greeting, both spoken and on official letters to Saudi officials. It's interesting to see the changes in the atmosphere, even on the streets. Today, a car next to us noticed we were Americans. And despite the fact I was a woman the Saudis gave me a thumbs up and waved a small American flag.

We continued to work sustainability issues to support the on-going peace effort. Also some work on the redeployment of troops and material. As during the actual deployment, and "war" I spent more time answering personal letters received by Gen. (Norman) Schwarzkopf regarding logistics issues such as the one received from "Granny Norris" as to why she had to send duct tape to her grandson to keep the sand out of his boots.

April 8—(letter) Surprise, surprise: CENTCOM actually had an official day off yesterday. As you can figure, the pool was crowded. I spent a little time there, and the rest shopping, sightseeing or snoozing. Latest rumor is that we are traveling with the CINC (commander-in-chief), and he has a penciled annotation on his calendar that he is departing the 18th.

Tichelaar did return home but was later assigned to Bahrain as a supply officer where she met her husband and-to-be, David Silverman. She and her husband, both retired, live in Comfort, Texas.

###

James R. Castleton:

Going in Harm's Way for
<u>God and Country</u>

James Robert "Jumby" Castleton is a transplanted Texan who graduated from the U.S. Naval Academy in 1985, during a period of relative peace in the world.

After earning his Wings of Gold as a naval flight officer, the Glendale, Arizona, native reported to his first squadron—VF-124—at NAS Miramar, California, for further training as a radar intercept officer (RIO) flying in the F-14 Tomcat. Little did he realize at the time that he would be putting his training to use during combat operations in just a few short years.

After qualifying as an RIO, Castleton reported for his first operational tour with the Bounty Hunters of VF-2, deployed aboard the USS Ranger (CV-61). Castleton was preparing for his second deployment aboard Ranger in late 1990 when he began to pick up signs that this deployment would be far different than his first one.

"My first cruise was standard Cold War WestPac (Western Pacific) fare," said Castleton, "but we knew going into December 1990, that this cruise was going to be anything but standard. That feeling was further confirmed when VF-2 Commanding Officer, A. J. "Action" Jackson, briefed the squadron just before the Thanksgiving holiday. He got our attention by giving us an hour-long brief on how we were leaving for the Gulf. It was his way of preparing us mentally," recalls Castleton. "The next indication of the seriousness of the situation was our departure. They craned our jets aboard the Ranger at NAS North Island.

"We spent the holidays in the Philippines and I remember being more concerned about what lay ahead than missing the Christmas and New Year's festivities back home.

Ranger arrived in the Arabian Gulf, two days before the start of the war. I can clearly remember thinking that it was nuts to go through the Straits of Hormuz," Castleton, said. "We were 'wound a little tight' knowing, or at least thinking, something big was going to be happening real soon.

"However, we weren't distracted. We were very focused. It just so happened I was airborne on CAP (combat air patrol) over the Gulf as the war started. I saw the first Tomahawk launch. Its flames were highlighted against the black night and even blacker Gulf water. Of course it was not verified until we were back on deck.

"Actually, I think I heard that we were at war on CNN rather than from an intelligence officer. The ship was buzzing with activity such as strike planning and ordnance handling. I was flying with a 'nugget'—junior pilot—so I wasn't scheduled for the first couple of strikes. I was actually a little bummed thinking I was missing a lifetime opportunity, but I also remember the whites of the flight crew's eyes as they manned their jets.

"My first close-up action was a classic 'Murphy's Law' sort of day. We had lost an A-6 on one of the early strikes and the ship was getting indications that the crew might have survived. I was scheduled to fly a CAP mission with my 'nugget' pilot. Our flight lead went down (broke) on deck so the spare filled in. As we launched, our mission was changed to combat search and rescue (CSAR). The adrenaline was really starting to flow as I realized that I was now the mission commander of our flight."

"Before we could begin the search the aircraft had to top off with fuel. The weather was foggy with cloud layers above 40,000 feet. The tanker, a KC-135, was circling at 30,000 feet. The F-14A doesn't like to tank at that altitude and we coughed (stalled) an engine. The lead was anxious to get to the coast to commence the CSAR and left us in the middle of the Gulf trying to re-light our engine. We finally caught up with him just as he reached the coast.

"After 20 to 30 minutes of searching both visually and on the radios, we decide this wasn't going to be our day, so we turned away from the coast. We had eased our way into the coast while hiding in the clouds. The commander of the E-2 Hawkeye scanning the area, asked us to take one more look before departing the area. The thought of helping down crewmen outweighed the danger of the situation and we turned back. However, we lost the sanctuary of the clouds and this time we popped out of the clouds on top of the coast in clear sight of the enemy.

"Iraqi anti-aircraft fire suddenly filled the air. Fortunately we were flying a few thousand feet below the 15,000 feet air wing altitude and the AA rounds were going off above the aircraft. I called for an immediate abort and exited the area.

"That mission really spooked my junior pilot," Castleton recalled. "He was also receiving some pressure from home and he elected to be grounded for the rest of the war. I guess you never know how you are going to react in war until you're actually in combat,"

Castleton spent the rest of the war as a "floater," meaning he flew fighter escort on a handful of strikes out of reach of Iraqi anti-aircraft fire, although he could clearly see AA bursts.

"The most dangerous missions I flew were the daylight Tactical Reconnaissance (TARPS) sorties," Castleton said. "We were flying lower, so the AA was a much bigger factor. It was also harder to see the SAMs (surface-to-air missiles). But the reconnaissance flights were well worth the risk. We figured out a way to use our imagery in almost real time so the A-6s could plunk the targets that we found."

For his 40 plus missions during the Gulf War, Castleton was awarded the Navy/Marine Commendation Medal with Combat V for the TARPS missions, and a Strike Flight Air Medal.

"The Ranger stayed in the Gulf until the conclusion of the War," Castleton said.

"Many of us were lucky enough to have our wives visit us in Thailand and Hong Kong. Those port visits are very memorable and will probably stick with me far longer than the details of the combat missions I flew.

"I personally believe I matured more on that cruise than during any other period in my life. I look back and remember the importance of training, confidence, and experience. Unfortunately, you can't gain true war experience without being in combat. I also realize that we (the Ranger and its air group) were lucky, or unlucky, depending on your point of view, to be one of the four carriers on station.

"Finally," Castleton says, "I remember the warmth and love of a nation as we returned. But I also feel that we celebrated too long. The only thing more amazing was the solidarity of the Coalition. Unfortunately, the warm relationship we had with many of the Coalition members has cooled considerably.

I learned that adversity can bring a nation together as in World War II, or tear it apart as it did with Vietnam.

"I feel fortunate to have been part of a positive experience while serving my God and country."

###

Clif Roberts:

<u>A Letter from the Desert</u>

During the preparation of this book, participating veterans told their stories in several different formats, including excerpts from a diary the authors received by e-mail. The following story detailing retired Master Chief Clif Roberts role in the Gulf War was taken from a news letter he sent home while serving as Force Master Chief for the Navy Logistics Force (NavSupFor).

"Hello from Bahrain, 250 miles from the Kuwaiti border.

"Well, I arrived in country on February 3, 1991, after helping put my ship, USS Tattnall (DDG-19), to sleep. Part of the decommissioning of the ship was the retirement of two of the most splendid warriors I've ever known, Commander Bill Fund, the commanding officer and Lieutenant Commander Paul Jones, the executive officer.

"Tears rolled down my cheeks as they sounded 'retreat' on the bugle and hauled down her ensign. What a ship, what a captain, executive officer and crew!

"Thanks so much for the thoughtful calls. Some war, when you can talk to your cousin in Monroe, Michigan, like he is next door. Sure long for all of you and I'm looking forward to seeing my old friends soon. Your patronage has been renowned and your camaraderie as always superior.

As 300 of us arrived on a 727, the pilot instructed us to go to MOPP (chemical biological warfare suit) condition II—don your gas mask. I did, rapidly. Bahrain was under a SCUD missile attack. For the next 21 days Saddam hurled about three missiles a night at us, normally at 2, 3 and 4 a.m. I assume he wanted to ensure we didn't sleep too well. Unfortunately, he got lucky a couple of times—damnit!

I'll never forget the night his missiles hit the barracks at Daharan which is right across the channel from us. I could feel the explosion.

Twenty-eight Americans gave their all that night. May the good Lord look after their souls.

Since arriving I've visited all three of our fleet hospitals, the harbor defense commands, cargo handling battalions and the hospital ships. I've visited 25 of the American ships that have put into Bahrain for one reason or another. I routinely travel with the admiral. Sometimes by plane, helicopter, fast patrol boat, armored car or jeep. But there are many occasions when my cohort, Chief Petty Officer Jerry Grace, and I travel about by ourselves. I report my findings from these trips back to the admiral and a lot of his personnel decisions are based on my conclusions.

The objective of these visits is always the same, to check out the morale, welfare, discipline, and training level of the men and women who are serving so honorably and professionally. They don't ask for much and they certainly cherish the marvelous support you're giving them back home. Thank you! Please keep it up.

The port cities of Ash Shuaybah, Kuwait; Al Jabayl, Al Dammam, Saudi Arabia; and Fujairah/Sharjak/Jebel Ah, United Arab Emirates, and Bahrain have been my stomping grounds. I've seen the projection of power this team of ours can bring to bear and I'm proud to report to you that we have defeated the fourth largest military in the world. I have seen destruction of equipment and buildings I never thought possible. It seems routine for thankful Kuwaitis to hug and kiss us for liberating them from beatings, rape, torture and executions.

The Iraqi soldiers, airmen and sailors surrender their weapons without firing a shot. I suppose the around-the-clock bombings destroyed their will to fight. I've been aboard several ships which the Iraqis captured from Kuwait. Our aviators, flying low-level attack runs, had all but destroyed the ships.

My choice to volunteer for the assignment was a conscientious one. I'll always be proud that I did. When I retire (June 28, 1991) after 32 years service, I will be able to say I had taken part in two hostile conflicts—the Cuba Blockade and Desert Storm—and we won both of them. It's always nice for a warrior to say I'm leaving in peace.

If I could have but one dream come true, it would be to attend the decommissioning ceremony of the final warship in the U.S. Navy. For then, I would know that the world was truly at peace and I had made a contribution.

I've discovered a lot about unified operations during my tour here. We had more than 115 Allied ships in the Persian Gulf at one time. I also discovered that there are numerous mines out there too. I've been on board USS Princeton and USS Tripoli and have seen what a 400 pound mine can to a capital warship It's awesome... eternal vigilance is the price of safety.

We deal with about 600,000 pounds of cargo, 500 passengers and 60,000 pounds of mail each day, from six logistic support ports. As you know, our Navy operates on beans, bullets and black oil. It is this command's responsibility to assure they are consistently abundant.

My duties over here are about to come to an end and I look forward to a happy and heartfelt homecoming with my lady in waiting, our children, grandchildren, and friends.

I will never forget this war and I'll always take pride in my service here. At the same time I'll always have great sympathy for those that won't be returning with me. They are the heroes. They paid for freedom with their lives.

###

Joel Norman:

Citizen Soldiers

Under the leadership of (then) Colonel Joel Norman, the 226 Area Support Group, Army National Guard, Mobile, Alabama, activated and deployed to Fort Rucker, Alabama, for two weeks in October 1990. Two weeks later the "Citizen Soldiers" were in Dhahran, Saudi Arabia.

"Our job during the war was to build logistics bases for the VII Corps and XVIII Airborne Corps before they started their in-sweep," Norman said. "Our mission was to provide support for the ground-gaining forces. We did this war a little different than we normally do. Normally, you have your combat troops out first, but in this war they put the logistics ahead of the combat arms."

After arriving in Dhahran, Norman met with Lieutenant General "Gus" Pagonis, the active duty Army general who was responsible for all logistics activities in the area.

"We found out the VII Corps was coming, so Pagonis decided to send our group north to King Khalid Military City (KKMC). I flew the area between KKMC and Hafar Al Batin (60 miles south of the Iraqi border) with the general and he gave me circles on the ground and said, 'This is where I want the VII Corps to go and this is where I want the logistics base built.'

Norman then flew back to Dhahran and began moving the majority of his troops to KKMC, with a smaller number setting up in Hafar Al Batin. Norman said his unit's job was to receive troops and provide them with food, water, fuel, building materials and spare parts for tanks and vehicles. The unit was also responsible for storing ammunition and grave registration.

"We were kind of like a Wal-Mart Super Store with what we provided." He laughed, "We were the landlords. When people moved in, we told them where to set up. Another part of the logistics operation was providing hot meals for the soldiers who were moving north.

We had 300,000 people there, so I was looking at close to a million meals a day," Norman said.

Norman said neither he, nor anyone else at the time had any idea of how long the war would last, so their goal was to have enough supplies on hand to care for these soldiers for two months.

The "Citizen Soldiers" were also confronted with the problem of supplying water for those 300,000 troops. Norman laughed and said, "You can have enough water in bottles to last a few days, but after that, you have to find a water supply in the desert—and that's kind of hard to do. You don't have a lot of engineers who can drill wells. When you're the first ones there you have to find out where to drill.

"We also had to provide storage for water as well as purification. We stayed busy, we stayed real busy."

"We had figured on losing 2,000 troops the first day," Norman said, "so we were trying to get refers (refrigerated trailers), body bags and ice. I had a grave registration unit that belonged to me. If we would have had the casualties we were expecting, it would have been the grave registration unit's responsibility to put them in body bags and keep them cool until we could get them back home—it was very intense.

"A system had to be worked out so that as bodies came in they could be searched to remove not only their personal items which were to be returned to the family, but to search them for hand grenades. You don't want to send a hand grenade home with a body," Norman said. He added that an Allied unit did have that problem.

With a sigh of relief, Norman continued, "I was happy to see the air war continue, because I knew the longer the air war continued the greater our chances of winning the war with fewer casualties.'

The day the bombing started, according to Norman, his unit began loading tanks for the two Army corps onto heavy equipment transports and began moving them to the positions from which the tanks would launch their attack. It took two weeks to complete the job.

"With both corps supplied, they were ready to kick the war off. The day we did the least amount of work was the day the ground war started because everything had been done. We're sitting back, just waiting to see what our jobs would be. Would it be to resupply? Would it be to take casualties back? The first day was just waiting, because we just didn't know what the future held for us.

Norman said the logistics set-up was only a short distance south of the Iraqi border. And because logistics went in first, there was no combat support. A few Special Forces observers were their only protection until the troops began to move in. Norman said his people were nervous about the situation, so he had buses brought in. If Iraq attacked before the troops arrived; their only option would be to load up on the buses and go south.

The Citizen Soldiers also had to deal with problems such as not having forklifts, building latrines and solid waste disposal, and building a landfill to support the trash problem for the more than 300,000 troops. After the war began, Norman said, "The first thing that happened was that the XVIII Airborne Corps' well went dry, so they didn't have any water. The only way to get water to the XVIII was to haul it. So the 226th had to load large rubber bladders onto flatbed trucks, fill them with water and haul it to them."

The war only lasted 100 hours, so in a few short days the logistics mission changed. In addition to continuing to provide support for the troops, the 226th also begin packing everything to be sent back to the United States.

The problems ended in June 1991 when Norman and his 5,000 troops returned home.

Norman said that one-month before his unit deployed, his twin sons, Wayne and Wesley, entered basic training. The medical unit the twins were to be assigned to after basic training did deploy to the Middle East. But the two young Norman's were still in basic training, which allowed them to bypass the war, but the fact that the boys were in recruit training, did little to ease the concerns of their mom, Jeannette, and their sister, Rachel.

Norman began his career with the Alabama Army National Guard as a private in 1957. He attended OCS and was commissioned a second lieutenant in 1961. In 1993 Colonel Joel Norman was promoted to brigadier general and placed in command of the 31st Armor Brigade at Tuscaloosa, Alabama. In 1997 he was promoted to major general and served as commander of the Alabama Troop Command in Montgomery.

After serving with the National Guard for more than 42 years, General Norman retired in 1999.

###

EPILOGUE

Ten years after the United States and its Allies had defeated, what at the time was reportedly the world's fourth largest Army—Iraq—America was once again fully engaged in armed conflict.

On September 11, 2001, terrorists, backed by the Islamic extremist Osama bin Laden, hijacked four commercial airliners. Two of the aircraft were crashed into the World Trade Center in New York City, completely destroying the twin towers and killing more than 3,000 people. A third plane crashed into the Pentagon in Washington, D.C., killing 189 people. The fourth airliner crashed into the Pennsylvania countryside killing all 45 people aboard, including the hijackers.

For years Afghanistan, with the blessing of its Taliban government, had been a training ground and safe harbor for bin Laden and his al Qaeda terrorists. When the Taliban refused to surrender Osama bin Laden and his chief deputies; the United States and Great Britain on October 7, 2001, launched Operation Enduring Freedom, a massive retaliatory strike against Afghanistan and bin Laden's al Qaeda network.

Within weeks of the first retaliatory strikes Afghanistan's Taliban government had been destroyed and Osama bin Laden, believed to be the mastermind for the September sneak attack on the American homeland, was on the run. After a decade-long manhunt Osama bin Laden's reign of terror ended, May 2, 2011, when he was discovered hiding in Abbottabad, Pakistan and killed during a firefight with members of the U.S. Navy's elite special forces SEAL Team Six,

On March 20, 2003, American returned to Iraq to, according to the United States and its Allies, "disarm Iraq of its weapons of mass destruction and to end Saddam Hussein's alleged support for terrorism."

Prior to the invasion, the governments of the United States and the United Kingdom asserted that in 2002, the United Nations Security Council passed Resolution 1441 which called for Iraq to allow UN weapon inspectors to verify that it was not in possession of weapons of mass destruction. The United Nations Monitoring, Verification and Inspection Commission were given access by Iraq under provisions of the UN resolution but no evidence of weapons of mass destruction has ever been found.

Despite this fact, however, more than a decade after the commencement of Operation Enduring Freedom American troops were still fighting and dying in Afghanistan and Iraq.

Made in the USA
Charleston, SC
26 November 2012